I Belong Here

Living the Life I was Born for in America

Helen H. Yee

ARMATURE PUBLISHING
Providing A Framework For The Language of the Soul

© 2022 by Helen H. Yee

ISBN: 979-8-9857738-0-4

No part of this book may be reproduced, stored in a retrieval system, or transmitted in any form or by any means—electronic, photocopy, recording—without prior written permission from Armature Publishing.

Cover artwork by Helen H. Yee
Cover design by Natalia Zukerman

Armature Publishing
c/o Lisa Ferraro
PO Box 254
Worthington, OH 43085
www.armaturepublishing.com
armaturepublishing@gmail.com

Contents

Chapter 1

"The Best Fight is No Fight"
~ Bruce Lee

Sliding my guitar case across the back seat of my BMW, I'm riding a wave of good vibes from a jam session. I've just finished practice with my band, Wednesday Wine, in our favorite venue. After the usual banter over drinks, I declined dinner in favor of a few quiet moments before turning in for the night.

I drive home, reviewing my performance in my head, humming the refrain from one of the songs we'd played. A deep feeling of contentment spreads over me like a warm summer night. The sun has sunk below the horizon, threatening the city with deepening shadows. It's barely 10 p.m. on a chilly spring weeknight. I'm looking forward to winding down.

Cars line both sides of my street. I pull into my driveway. A car drives past. I check that I have my phone on me. I pull my keys from the ignition. To retrieve the guitar from the back seat, I press the button on my keys to unlock the back doors. Suddenly the front passenger door flies open. A man in a hoodie invades the seat next to me, a bandanna over his face and mouth. He's very physically fit, bigger, and stronger than me. At four foot eleven, I'm no match for him.

"I need you to drive me somewhere," he says, calm as can be.

Then I see the gun pointing at me. *Ohmygod!*

My whole being sinks to the ground. There's no time to panic. I'm a third-degree black belt—what's my strategy?

"Okay," I say. *I am not going anywhere with him,* my strategy says. The butterflies calm. Suddenly I know my plan. Instantly I feel centered, at peace. Whatever happens is going to happen right here, in my neighborhood. Then, I look at him. "Hey, I know you." It totally startles him. He's trying to disguise his identity.

"No, you don't!"

"Yeah, you're Darrin's friend," I say. I don't even know a Darrin. This comment totally flips him out. Meanwhile, my knee presses against the car door.

"Just drive!" he says, more sternly.

"Okay."

My strategy is to play along. I put the keys near the ignition. Abruptly, I launch myself out of the car and run. I'm small and fast.

Use your voice! my head says. I'm not used to screaming. I've never had to do this. Even if there's nobody around, your screaming may startle the assailant enough to leave. In self-defense class, these are my words to students. My instructor's words to me. Finally, I find my voice.

"HELP! HELP!" I scream.

I dash to my neighbor's house across the street. I keep my eyes forward. I don't know where the masked man is. If he shoots me, it will be in my back, on my street. I bang on the door. I don't wait for an answer. I then run to hide because I don't know where he is. The yard of my next-door neighbor offers no cover. But I see his car. Quickly I flatten myself out and slide underneath. At least if the gunman is still chasing me, I'll be able to see his feet. Remembering my phone, I pull it out, and dial another neighbor. No answer.

"Dammit!" I hang up and shut off the screen, afraid it's illuminating my face, giving away my location. A moment later, I speed dial my business partner, Michelle.

"Hello?"

"Uh, yeah. Call the police! I've just been held up at gunpoint!" I hang up. I don't want the gunman to overhear me.

In the movies, the good guys win, and the bad guys get caught; the martial artist leaps into a series of gravity defying kicks and punches, which incapacitates the bad guy, breaks his nose, and sends his gun skittering out of reach. But this is not a movie. It's real life in Columbus, Ohio, on a spring night. I'm hiding from a gunman who threatened me in my own car. My mind speeds through questions. *What will happen next? Will I live to see another day? Will help arrive in time?* There is still so much I want to do with my life. The only person who knows I'm in trouble may not even be sure where I called from: Home? Work? Or somewhere else. In the adrenaline rush, I forgot to tell her my location. I know Michelle well enough to know that she will call the police. We'd been through a lot together—life, love, and business—and had a good relationship.

Under my neighbor's car, all sense of time vanishes. I don't know if anyone else heard my screams. I haven't seen any trace of the gunman for what seems like a long time. I strain my ears for approaching footsteps, for any telltale sound indicating I am not alone. My focus is laser sharp, and I only want to get through this.

Of all the wild and daring adventures I've had across the globe up to this point, it's ironic that I'm facing death in my own neighborhood within yards of my front door. *Did he target me because I projected some sense of vulnerability? Or was I just some random woman? Did he choose me because of the way I look?*

The martial arts tactics I have learned are, for the present, keeping me alive. Another irony. The Asian heritage I shunned, tried to cast off, and worked so hard to eradicate in my youth is now protecting me. The path I chose in response to experiencing racism and bullying has mentally prepared me to act correctly in this white-hot moment of time. Later I will realize, had I not listened to that inner voice, this night could have turned out very differently. I might have caved at his harsh words, turned the key in the ignition, and been hurtling down the highway toward a deserted location, pleading for my life.

This is a story of how bullying impacted my life, the ironic choice that changed my trajectory, and how the lessons learned paved the way for a fulfilling, successful future. My story is about living in the present moment and being in the now. It is the only moment that truly matters.

Chapter 2

My Family History

My first memory is being about two years old. My grandmother was holding me up to a faucet and washing my little hands underneath cold running water. Then she put me in a big metal tub with soapy, milky-looking water. I can still smell the soap. I was facing my brother. I was surrounded by all these loud voices—because Chinese people talk very loudly. I was feeling loved by my grandparents, my mom, and especially my grandmother. The aroma of delicious food wafted in from the kitchen: Chinese sausage, bitter melon, and stuffed tofu. Though I didn't know it yet, food is one of the linchpins of our family.

The city of Hong Kong could be likened to Manhattan, in that there's not a whole lot of real estate to be had. You don't just buy a house. What you get there is a single-family unit, a flat in a high-rise building. I'm sure we all lived with my mother's mother and father: my mother and father, two older brothers, and me. My parents were already dreaming of another life outside of Hong Kong and had been for many years. They had their sights set on America.

The men of the Yee family already had a long history of emigrating to various cities in the United States. In 1885, Jin Jang Yee, my great-great-grandfather, landed in San Francisco and worked on the railroad, as well as mining and farming. While delivering produce in San Francisco, he was killed in a horse-cart accident. Chinese custom dictated that the deceased must be returned to the homeland. His son (my great-grandfather) went to San Francisco to carry out this task. Later, in 1895, he immigrated to Phoenix, Arizona, and started a grocery store, sending support to his wife and children in China. On November 5, 1900, George (my grandfather) was born in Ton Shan, Guangdong Province, China. He was one of four children his mother raised by herself, a common practice in those days, while their husbands worked in America. George attended elementary school and high school and learned English skillfully enough to teach others. He later married, had two sons, and supported the family by teaching. In 1921, on his first attempt to emigrate, he replied incorrectly to a question. As a result, he was jailed and sent back to China. The following year, he successfully joined his father in Phoenix. Instead of helping his father in his grocery store, George performed farm work, which he didn't like. He spoke excellent English, which afforded him different opportunities. He moved to Columbus, Ohio, to work in a restaurant.

George faithfully sent money back to his family as often as he was able. To my understanding, he returned to China in 1927 and two more children were born. In 1937, George came back to Columbus, and he and a partner opened their own restaurant, Far East. George managed the front-of-house and tended bar, while his partner was head chef. From San Francisco they imported weekly grocery shipments with hard to find items such as fresh mushrooms, wonton and spring roll wraps, and snow peas. In the kitchen, they grew their own bean sprouts. They hired fine cooks from Chicago and New York. Soon they outgrew their building and expanded to a new, larger space. He continued sending money home for his children's education, enabling his wife to buy houses and land.

He visited China again in early 1937. Now, he owned some property with three or four houses on it. When the Japanese invaded Nanking in December 1937, it is believed George's property was taken. Unfortunately, the property deed has not been found. George also sent money to the Chinese government to help the war effort against Japan. Due to immigration laws and wartime, he was prevented from returning to China for twenty years. This same war prevented him from communicating with his family from 1940 to 1945. The year after the war ended, my grandfather sponsored the immigration of his nephew (my uncle), Wayne Yee, and put him to work at Far East.

Forty years after George landed in the United States, my grandfather was able to sponsor his wife, Ying Ma, his son, Peter (Sum Yin) Yee—my father—along with my mother, Nora (Lai Yuk), my two brothers, Tom and Bob, and me. We arrived in Columbus, Ohio from Hong Kong in 1962 and lived with Grandfather in the first house that he'd purchased on Enfield Road. It wasn't too far from the school I would later attend with my younger brother, Henry, who was born after we arrived in America.

After many years in the restaurant business together, Grandfather and his partner went their separate ways. I was too young to understand the significance of this event, or the impact it would have on my life. However, whether I knew it or not, I would soon be absorbing principles that would serve me throughout my life from someone I would hold in high esteem long after I grew up.

In adapting to new customs and a new way of life in a new country, my grandfather and many other immigrants kept their focus on their dream of a better life here for themselves and for their families. Although my grandfather was fluent in English, for many Chinese people English was a brand new language. As if that weren't challenging enough, they had to overcome cultural and racial prejudices. The hate and aggression many Asians experienced resulted in frustration and despair. These challenges were just some of the obstacles they experienced as they adjusted to life here in America.

Chapter 3

George & Ying Ma
in the Midwest

My grandfather opened his second restaurant, Yee's Restaurant, in 1967. The menu featured both Chinese and Western-style dishes. Yee's became the family business, where Grandfather, Father, Mother, and Uncle Wayne all worked. Because of his strong work ethic, many of the cooks from Far East came to work with us. A few of his former employees even started their own restaurants. He sponsored a number of his friends from China so they could enjoy a better life. Later, they were able to bring their families to this country. George Yee was well loved because of the way he treated folks. He regarded everyone with dignity and respect, and in return, they responded the same toward him. He knew how to connect with people and engage them in wonderful conversations.

As a role model to me in many ways, I watched how my grandfather lived and enjoyed his life, not so much his words but how he conducted himself at home, at work with employees, and with friends and family. He was consistent in his personal integrity, in his business, and in his exercise. Even though (as a child) I didn't have any interest in doing Tai Chi or Qigong, he practiced every day. As a dedicated musician, he played several kinds of flutes and the *erhu*, which is sometimes called a spike fiddle, with two strings. His joy of playing led him to form his own small band. I still have all his Chinese instruments, which I remember hearing him play. Because of this, I also found joy and refuge in music.

My grandfather and both of my parents spoke English, but my dad didn't speak it very well. My parents also spoke different dialects of Chinese. Mom spoke both languages very well. My oldest brother, Tom, who was ten years older than me, could speak Chinese and understand it. My brother Bob was a year younger than Tom; he understood and spoke a bit of Chinese, but not as well as Tom. When I was younger, I understood more of what Mom said, but it was harder understanding Dad.

My dad was a happy, fun-loving guy, a free spirit. He had some very different ideas, but he taught me how to have fun in life. He once got hold of a cicada, tied a thread on it, and tied the other end to a rubber tree plant in the living room. It could still fly around, even though it was captive. I came home from school that day and heard this weird cricket noise. *What the heck? It sounds so close!* I turned and saw this tethered cicada flying right where I needed to go. I'm like, "Oh my God!" The thread was just long enough that I couldn't pass to the hall where my bedroom was. Dad was in the living room watching. "I need to get to my room!" I said, probably two octaves higher than normal. "And you've got this huge cockroach flying around!"

"It's for good luck!" he laughed.

Even though sons typically have higher status in Chinese families, I felt very loved. Being my dad's only daughter, I was Dad's favorite, and we had our own unique connection. Before I went to school, my dad was a big encourager of my creativity, especially art. I drew birds and animals for him, which he always enjoyed. My dad came from the tradition that fathers were not the disciplinarian. This may have stemmed from his father (and his father's father) working overseas in America for months and years at a time, leaving their wives to raise children on their own. Usually, if Dad had a beef with one of us kids, he told Mom and she came to us to explain what we had done wrong or how we had behaved improperly. Like the time at dinner, when I was feeding our dog, Whitey, under the table. He was eating so loudly that I pretended it was me making the loud smacking noises. But my parents weren't fooled. After dinner, she made me kneel in the corner of the room and hold on to my earlobes until she was ready to release me. Even though this form of punishment was typical of Chinese mothers, and considered mild (and very effective), Mom was unhappy about being the disciplinarian. My dad was more of a supporter and encouraged my athletic abilities in various sports—although I think he wanted me to be a swimmer. He even got us a pool pass. He always watched when I dove off the high dive. He'd be waiting for me to come up for air. The second my head broke the water, he'd critique my form, offering unasked-for pointers. His assessments took the fun out of it.

Despite these corrections, only one time do I remember my dad disciplining me—and justifiably so. I was about eight. I was sitting on the floor in the room I shared with Henry. He was asleep on his bed, and I was between him and my bed, striking matches. All of a sudden, I heard footsteps coming down the hallway. Thinking to blow out the matches, I quickly threw them under Henry's bed. I pretended to be doing nothing until they went past my door. Then I looked under the bed. The whole bottom of it was on fire!

I hurried to the bathroom and grabbed the cup on the sink and filled it with water. So as not to attract attention, I walked nonchalantly down the hall until I got to my bedroom. I sprinted to the bed, attempting to throw enough water to put out the fire. Henry was still asleep on his bed. Somehow, divine intervention helped me put the fire out. Whew!

Then my dad came walking by, sniffing the air. He poked his head in our room.

"Hey, what is that smell?"

"What smell?" I asked.

"It smells like smoke."

I pretended to look around. Nervously, I pointed toward the open window, hoping my dad would simply go out there to check. "I think the smell might be coming in the window, from outside."

If he left, maybe the smell would dissipate enough that I'd still manage to get off the hook. Undeterred, my dad followed his nose, which brought him into my room. He knelt in the space between our beds and looked under my bed, seeing nothing. But then he looked under Henry's bed. When he saw how burned up the bottom of it was, he didn't even have words for me. His eyes flew open wide. He grabbed me by the ankles and stood, holding me upside down. He was so upset and angry he cursed me in Chinese. I had no idea what he was saying, but I knew he was very upset, and his reaction made clear to me that playing with matches was dangerous.

He didn't hit me, but he was terrified of what could have happened. That was the first time he had ever attempted discipline. Despite that incident, our relationship remained unchanged. He continued taking me places and doing fun things together, just the two of us.

It didn't help my relationship with Mom that Dad preferred to have fun and do things with me, leaving her out. This made her envious of our relationship. Her envy was a very real thing. If I thought about how she felt about me at all, I would have said she was typical of most Chinese mothers. However, one of my childhood friends confirmed this years later during one of our phone conversations. She mentioned that my mom was very hard on me and seemed jealous of me. I didn't feel unloved by Mom, I just felt more favored by Dad. When Henry came along a year after me, he became her favorite. He never had to do chores. She spoiled him by letting him get away with everything.

Both my parents worked long hours at the restaurant; Mom came home late most nights just ahead of him. At one or two o'clock in the morning, she started cooking dinner for my dad, knowing he would be home soon. I loved my mom's amazing cooking! So much so that when the smell of food drifted into my bedroom and woke me, I'd get up and go downstairs. I'd sit at the table half asleep eating dinner with them. Those are some of my favorite memories.

My dad worked very hard at the restaurant. For fun, he liked to go fishing. At some point, he was inspired to create a nautical theme in the bar at Yee's. He hung fish netting up then bought a bunch of sea things: big starfish, porcupine fishes, sea urchins, anything that went with the ocean theme, and he tossed it up into the net.

He also liked gambling and taking trips to Las Vegas, where they treated him very well. God knows how much money he really lost. (This, of course, was never discussed in front of us when we were growing up.) He was also a little eccentric. His mind was constantly working to find easier ways to do things. For example, the back seat locks in his Cadillac didn't unlock. Rather than going to a pricey repair shop to get them fixed, he tied twine to the pin knobs and rigged it so that while he sat in the driver's seat, he could just pull the twine to unlock the door.

He was a great match for my mom, who was a chain smoker, animated, and very spicy. It seems like everyone smoked back then. We were out in public somewhere and she was seated at a table. She had just put her cigarette out. Some guy was standing too close to her, talking to another person, waving his hand all about with a lit cigarette. She looked at me and said something like, "So help me if he burns me with his cigarette, he's going to be very sorry!" Lucky for him, it never touched her.

My mom wasn't a gambler, but she loved playing the Asian tile-based game *mah-jongg*—and she played a lot! She and her friends got together on a regular basis and brought their kids with them. They were from different locations all around Columbus. Sometimes they came over and had dinner at our house, sometimes we went to theirs. They played until all hours of the night—up until five or six in the morning. The kids were my age, and we did everything together and spent the night wherever our moms played. Us kids sometimes pretended we were a rock band. This was my community growing up. We all looked the same, talked the same, played the same games, and ate the same food—everything in our lives was the same. The kids lived all over Columbus and went to schools in their own neighborhoods.

I went to kindergarten at Fairmoor, a public school, and I wasn't the least bit afraid of going. I felt happy being in this big fun room for half a day to play with blocks or crayons and other kids. Although I don't remember, I'm certain there must have been other Asian kids there.

When I went to first grade at St. Catharine's, it seemed stricter and more structured. My mom led me down a hall to my classroom. Inside was a very tall nun named Sister Ann. She stood in front of the class dressed in a habit of long, white robes. All the students sat very quietly at their desks. It was then, standing at the front of that class, that I noticed. Nobody in there looked like me.

For the first time, I realized this incredible difference not only in the way I looked, but how they looked. How different their language was, their odors, their clothing, and their mannerisms. The newness of being in a situation like that—a completely non-Asian environment and not knowing anyone—suddenly overwhelmed and terrified me. Lynette, who became one of my first-grade friends, reminded me how frightened I was. She said I had grabbed on to my mom's leg, crying, and hung on for dear life. My mom literally dragged me across the linoleum as she tried to get out of the room. Lynette remembered thinking, *Gosh, let her go! Just let her go home with her mom.* But Mom left me there. It didn't take long for the kids to begin pointing out how I was different from them. It made me feel embarrassed and ashamed and that I wasn't like them. I equated being Chinese with being less than. It wasn't enough to be myself.

My parents were deeply traditional and wanted us to hang on to our culture. My older brothers didn't want to have any part in it. Once I began attending school, I understood why: our style of life was distinct from the people around us. My parent's upbringing was very different—they grew up in China where it was right and expected for one to be proud of their ancestry and traditions. But that was what everyone around them did—and the society around them reinforced those values. Outside of our home, those reinforcements didn't exist. My parents' cultural norms were not the norms of Midwestern America in the 1960s. Mom had grown up in a sea of her own people. We kids were alone in another sea.

Aside from Fred, the person that I hung out with most was Lynette. She and I were friends from first grade to high school graduation. We rode bikes together and had sleepovers, mostly at her house. One time early in our friendship, she came to my house and overheard my parents talking to some of their friends in Chinese. With wide eyes, she asked, "Are they mad at each other?" referring to their boisterous and animated discussion.

"Huh? Oh, no, that's normal."

Obviously, it wasn't normal to her. She was terrified because they talked so loudly; to her, it sounded like they were screaming at each other!

I enjoyed spending time at her house because her parents were the coolest parents ever, and they really knew how to have a lot of fun. I always felt welcome there. In some ways, my life was very Asian and in other ways it wasn't, like at lunchtime. Mom sent me and Henry to school with packed lunches—but they weren't your typical PB&J. They were huge club sandwiches, or veal parmesan, or something out of this world. The other kids always crowded around me to see what surprise I had in my lunch box—and then offered to trade. This made me slightly popular at lunch. "What have you got there?" I'd ask. "Chip-chop ham? Ugh, no . . . What do you have?" I'd ask, scanning all the different offerings. I could afford to be picky and was always interested in seeing if I could trade up to something better.

The parts of school that I liked, which made school more bearable, were less predictable. My love of drawing and coloring made any kind of art project or even science project something to look forward to. It turns out that I had one talent that most of the kids in my class didn't—artistic ability. Fortunately, this was something they held in high regard. In third or fourth grade art class, the other kids made a point to see what I drew or painted. Another boy in my class, named Robert, was also artistic. My classmates always wanted to see what we created, and then they'd compare our work to see who they thought was more creative or whose drawing looked better. For a Christmas project, two other girls teamed up with me and we made a Rudolph the Red-Nosed

Reindeer piñata out of aluminum foil—just to be different—and then glued all kinds of stuff on it. It occurs to me now that the character Rudolph was also ostracized by his peers because of a physical difference. Hoping to avoid the jeering of his peers, Rudolph also tried blending in by covering his unique glowing nose. Only much later would he figure out that he had a special gift. Someone very special would call upon that glowing nose to navigate through a particularly bad storm, much to the awe of all his friends.

Because this lesson escaped me at the time, I was still trying to figure out when and under what circumstances being different was acceptable. Many times, I was teased about my looks. Some kids made derogatory remarks or called me "Chink." It was worse for my brothers, who were in physical confrontations almost daily. Henry was always fighting with other boys. I didn't experience that level of physical altercations, but even as a girl, I was not exempt from them.

I got into a couple of physical fights, but most of the bullying directed at me was through name-calling. And even when it didn't occur every day, they still left their mark. The names were meant to be hurtful. It wore on me. It undermined me emotionally and psychologically. My guard was up constantly, and that's a lot for any kid to carry. Bullying incidences can sow seeds of hypervigilance, wondering when the next occurrence will happen. Initially, it makes you hesitant of going to new places or meeting new people because you constantly feel judged for your appearance. You can't forget who or what you are because someone is always there to remind you and make you feel like you're not good enough, not equal, not like them.

When things got to be too much, I had "safe places" I went to. One of my fondest childhood memories is climbing trees. I had a secret fort hidden in a bush. I kept some of my precious things in a plastic box in the fort. There was something empowering about climbing the huge maple tree behind our garage, in our neighbor's backyard. Especially when I'd reach the highest branches and I could see my house and all around. I'd just sit up in the branches and feel the breeze make them sway. I'd climb into the tree fort and play or read in a little made-up world of my own.

It seemed all the kids in our family were suffering from this silent thing called racism. And I would have thought feeling like the low man on the totem pole was the way it was always going to be. But soon, I was going to get an unexpected glimmer of hope.

Chapter 4

Bruce the Brat

Mom enrolled my older brothers at St. Charles, possibly thinking that a private school would be a better experience for them, or at least a better education. But after one semester they were like, "Forget this!" Instead, they attended Eastmoor, a pretty rough public school. Soon, they were getting into fights and getting beat up all the time. They survived by joining gangs, which protected them and gave them something to belong to. In grade school, there were no gangs. Because I was naturally athletic and competitive, the next best thing was joining a team. I tried out and was accepted on the basketball team and the softball team, and I also became a cheerleader. That was the beginning of wanting to belong to everything. I just wanted to be like *them*. As much as I wanted to, I couldn't change my looks. But when everyone is wearing the same uniform, there's a sense of blending in.

I wanted the approval of the people around me. As a way of trying to fit in, I went along with the crowd. It worked to a point, but it didn't prevent my being singled out off the field.

After school one day, instead of my mom waiting to pick me up, I saw my oldest brother, Tom, in the passenger seat of a very nice car. One of his friends was in the driver's seat. He had come to whisk me away from St. Catharine's! He was sixteen or seventeen at the time. As I ran toward him, he noticed I had been crying.

"What happened?"

"Nothing," I said.

"Get in," Tom said. I climbed into the back seat. I didn't know the friend who was driving. Tom was with the cool guys from his school, and they all wore leather jackets. I didn't want to cry in front of them. Tom turned around to look at me. "You don't cry about nothing. Just tell me what happened."

"Some stupid boy is making fun of me every day for no reason."

"I want you to point him out to me."

I scanned the kids milling around until I spotted the one who was making my life misery. "There," I said, pointing him out.

Tom leaned out the window and yelled. "Hey, kid! You! Come over here." The boy walked over. When he saw me in the back seat, he knew right away he was in big trouble. In that moment, I felt so proud of my brother and proud to be his little sister. I remember feeling safe and thinking, *Wow. My big brother is so cool!* The kid came closer, even though he was clearly afraid.

"If you ever make fun of my sister again," said Tom, "I will kill you." That boy never said another word to me or messed with me again.

Racism didn't come from just kids. My mother had taken Henry and me to SS Kresge. Inside was a little diner with a lunch counter and high-back stools that spun around. The menu consisted of sundaes, sandwiches, malted milkshakes, hamburgers and fries, drinks, and desserts. My mother liked to shop, and she would leave us at the counter where we could order something.

"I'll be back. Here's some money for a milkshake for you and your brother." We sat there and waited patiently for the waitress to take our order. She wasn't that busy, but she totally ignored us. Then it seemed clear she didn't intend to wait on us at all. When Mom finally came back, she looked at us with confusion on her face. "Didn't you guys want a milkshake?"

"Yeah, but the waitress won't wait on us," I said.

Very calmly, Mom went up to the waitress and handed her a bill. "Can you please get my children what they want?" My mother literally had to give the woman the money to wait on us. I remember that event partly because by now I was familiar with what racism felt like. Even though I had never witnessed my parents being targeted by racists, my mother's actions showed that she knew exactly what to do when such an event occurred.

After school, Henry and I didn't walk home together or ride with the other kids on the bus. Normally, one of our parents came to pick us up and then took us to Yee's, our family restaurant. In bar booths separate from the main dining area, we solved math problems, practiced our spelling, and grew up. While some romanticize the notion of having your own restaurant, it's actually a lot of boring work. As I got older, I played hostess: passing out menus, seating people, and bringing water to the table. Sometimes I helped in back with the dishes. Even though I love traditional Chinese food, I never wanted to be in the kitchen learning how to prepare or cook any of it. The kitchen, with steaming pots of boiling water, sizzling vats of oil, and knives so sharp they effortlessly sliced the hardest root vegetables, wasn't necessarily the safest place to be. My grandmother, George's wife, didn't speak any English. She was notorious for going into the kitchen and riling up the cooks with her caustic Chinese criticism. One day, one of the cooks had had enough.

"If you don't get out of here," he said, picking up his razor-sharp butcher knife, "I'm going to *jom-nee-ka-towlah!*" This means, "cut your head off," and it's considered a really bad phrase in Chinese—comparable to "fuck you." Needless to say, he wanted her out of the kitchen.

Yee's stayed open until one or two in the morning. My parents worked very late, which meant Henry and I often slept there until Mom was ready to leave for the night. Keeping us nearby was how they were able to run the business.

After middle school at St. Catharine's, I went to Bishop Hartley. Henry followed the same track. Pretty soon he was always in fights and getting beat up, the same thing that had happened to Tom and Bob. I'm sure my mother didn't want Henry following the path of the older two, which had led to gangs and, occasionally, police at the door. Henry was brilliant and what took me a lot of hard study to learn came easily to him. He didn't even have to try, but he went a different way and eventually got into drugs. In high school, I continued trying out for sports and playing on teams. My dad suggested I play volleyball, largely because of his experience as a volleyball coach when he was in Hong Kong. But I wanted to play field hockey. When I made the field hockey team, it might have been the first time Dad was disappointed that I wouldn't do something that he perceived he could help me with. After the joy had been sucked out of diving, I chose something he couldn't tell me how to perfect. Later, I played softball and joined the drill team. What I liked about being on the drill team was doing all the formations and feeling like we were performing with military precision. Without anyone to compare us to, I thought we were very cool.

The first time we went to a competition, we noticed all the other corps were scantily dressed and doing their routines along with popular tunes. We were the only corp without music. I remember thinking, *We're really way behind . . . . Man, we are not cool.* My parents didn't attend competitions or the games; not because they didn't want to, but because they worked relentlessly. They had their hands full running a successful business and getting my brother through school, despite the company he kept. At least I was (mostly) staying out of trouble.

Until I got my own car, the parents of teammates picked me up and dropped me off for practices and games. Afterward, I always got a ride home or to the restaurant. Instead of focusing on my lack of parental support in the stands, I was happy to be on a team and had fun with a small circle of friends who, for the most part, treated me like everyone else. Their parents cheered us on, and at the time that was enough for me. There were sometimes after-game celebration meals, and I was always invited along. The summer I turned sixteen I got my driver's license. For my birthday, my parents had bought me one of my favorite cars—an awesome pre-owned Plymouth Duster. Not everybody my age had their own vehicle.

One summer night, I was invited to a party at my friend Lynette's house, and I was excited about going over to hang out and have a few beers. Her parents were the hippies with money! Their home was a party house with some very cool features. In their huge backyard was a bridge over a koi pond, and inside they had installed an actual telephone booth! In the basement, black lights were installed in their ceiling which made the psychedelic designs painted on the walls glow brightly. I sat in one of the beanbag chairs while kids played pool. A mirrored disco ball spun from the ceiling, and some other kids boogied under it on the dance floor. I nervously played spin the bottle for the first time in the basement. I think it was everyone's first time!

After midnight, I drove home from the party. I was probably trying to get home before my mom did and was going too fast, definitely over the speed limit. Next thing I knew, I saw a police car coming toward me. He made a U-turn behind me and I thought, *Oh, dammit!* I didn't think about how much trouble I would actually be in if I got caught, I just thought, *I can't get caught!* Fueled by a little panic and a little daring, I hit the metal to the floor.

On the street near my house, there was a four-way stop with a big speed hump to slow down traffic. Because I was trying to get away and going too fast, when I hit that hump, all four wheels came off the ground. I flew over that intersection. The car hit bottom—BAM! But I kept going. This was my neighborhood, and I knew how to get around. As fast as I could, I swerved down one of the side roads. I parked, snapped off the headlights and held my breath. Sure enough, the police car traced my path with lights flashing and siren blaring. My blood was racing. *Oh my God, am I busted?* Then, he passed the street where I had parked.

I couldn't believe my good fortune! First hurdle done, one more to go. How was I going to get home without using my lights? I couldn't risk being seen by that police car. Surely, he was scouring the streets looking for me now. Carefully, I drove home by the light of streetlamps and hid the car behind our house right next to the garage. My adrenaline was still pumping. I couldn't believe I had outrun the police . . . and gotten away with it! Had I been caught, I would have been busted for not only underage drinking but fleeing from a police officer, driving over the speed limit, running a four-way stop, and maybe even DUI. Not to mention being out past curfew! That could have changed the trajectory of my whole life. That was not the direction that I wanted to go.

The next morning, my mom questioned me. "So why is your car parked out back?"

"Oh, I don't know," I said, pretending to be cool. I didn't even have an excuse and I couldn't tell her the truth. "I just felt like parking back there." If she knew anything more than that, she didn't say it. Had she known, I'm sure she would have said a lot.

In the spring before high school graduation, I had a decision to make. What was I going to do with my life? Restaurant work was easy, but I didn't want to spend my whole life there. There was a lot of talk amongst my friends about going off to college. If I decided to go, and my grades were good enough, I would be the first person in my family to attend. When it came to choosing a university and a major, who the hell knew what they wanted at that age? Out of all my friends, only one of them knew exactly what they wanted.

Barb was one of my closest friends in high school. We enjoyed many sleepovers and trips together and laughed a lot! Sometimes we would get into trouble at school for being late for algebra or Spanish class. This was usually after lunch. We also enjoyed playing field hockey together. When time for high school graduation rolled around, Barb said she was going to Ohio Dominican College (which has since become Ohio Dominican University). She contributed to my final decision, based solely on the most important criteria: I wanted to go because she was going there. I signed up for Fall classes thinking art was a talent I could utilize. I could always switch my major if it didn't work out.

After graduating from high school, I didn't want to work at the restaurant for free anymore. I decided to get my own job. I applied for a position at Cochrane's pharmacy, which was at the end of the strip mall, down from the restaurant—and they hired me! I really loved working there and had the best time because a lot of people who worked there were my age. But one day an older fellow came into the store, a Vietnam veteran. Something was definitely off with his mind. Everyone seemed to know him, and I learned he was a regular. When he looked at me, he called me "Charlie." He made other derogatory remarks about the Vietnamese and the Vietnam War.

Ahhh, God! I thought. Even in my new job, there was racism. It seemed I couldn't get away from it. The question was, what was I going to do about it? The female manager who witnessed the event stepped in immediately. She politely asked him to leave without making a scene. Then, she apologized to me for his behavior. That gesture touched me and was very meaningful. But that got me thinking: with high school finished, I could put my money into another kind of education. I decided to take Kung Fu classes, a Chinese martial art.

Interestingly, my mother and I both liked watching Kung Fu movies. She liked the ones with a love story, of course, and I had grown up watching and liking the ones with Bruce Lee. It was just so cool to watch his moves! Bruce Lee opened a door for me to reclaim a part of myself before it totally disappeared. Because of his skillful fighting, he made taking up self-defense attractive. The draw for me was doing the fancy kicks and being able to defend myself. I couldn't have known, at that time, the impact he would have in bringing martial arts to the United States. But mainly, he represented a part of my heritage. Bruce Lee was a person whom I looked up to as a hero and mentor. What's funny is my mother and I shared a polarizing passion for Bruce Lee. I liked him so much I hung a poster of him in my room.

"Ah *gawd*. You're kidding, right?" Mom said when she saw it. It turns out she hated Bruce Lee. "He was such a bully!" They had lived on the same street in Kowloon. My mom was slightly older than him. While she and her friends were standing together wearing their school uniforms, he came up and threw *char siu bao* at them, soiling their uniforms. He was just a kid, a typical brat long before he got into martial arts and became famous. We shared that common rebellion. (Did my mother not know I had done a similar thing when I was in Hong Kong?) But my mom

of English. In spite of language barriers, he created an amazing school in Columbus, Ohio. He developed several more schools in different states across the country and branches in Europe, Canada, and Mexico. He built a kind of empire. Although he expected a lot out of us, he was very dedicated.

I was so into martial arts that as soon as I finished my college classes or finished work, I went straight there practically every day. I took multiple classes and even went in early. In that kind of setting, you eventually work with all the instructors, or you can pay for private one-on-one lessons with a specific master or instructor. Just by being there all the time, I sometimes got one-on-one lessons with Master Choi or one of the other instructors. I dedicated a lot of my own time to learning because that's how I am. I didn't have my mom pushing me to succeed. She worked all the time. I became my own "Tiger Mom," the Chinese mother who pushes her kid to excel and be successful to the detriment of exhausting them. I definitely had a way of pushing myself. Initially, the main reason I signed up was to defend myself because I wanted to learn how to fight. However, martial arts became my saving grace. I soon learned that martial arts aren't just about physical skills. They are about strategy, building character, and strengthening virtues; they develop discipline, patience, respect, and honor. The practice is rich with culture, heritage, and tradition. Previously, in sports, I was one of the team. What we did, we all did as a group. If we succeeded, we succeeded as a team. If we failed, no one was singled out. But now I felt connected and supported on my individual merit.

I noticed that people were super respectful in class, which was so different from being in grade school. Many who get into martial arts have an admiration for not only the art and discipline but a strong respect for the Eastern and Asian culture. I sensed my classmate's deference immediately. For the first time, being Asian worked to my advantage. It was such an amazing experience to have people automatically respect you, even if you're just starting out, just for being Asian! I realized that instead of making fun of me for being Chinese, it was the reason

I was being respected. To say it was a delightful surprise is an understatement.

The most astonishing thing happened the first time I went to a tournament—people bowed to me . . . even though I hadn't made black belt yet! At first, I thought it was because, collectively, we are taught to respect all martial arts disciplines. Maybe they thought I was a master or something. It never occurred to me that they respected me simply *because* I was Chinese. After all I had been through in school, that was one of the most unexpected shifts. I wasn't just tolerated because I was one of the team. I was being accepted as Helen Yee, the person. Because others showed me respect, I became more accepting of myself. I finally felt more comfortable in my own skin and just being me. This allowed me to blossom as a person in my own right.

After training with my teammates, we'd go out and have fun. We enjoyed hanging out together, and I really felt like one of the gang. It was different than in high school, where after a game with the field hockey or softball team we'd go to Wendy's or some fast-food place. Back then, it was just fun to be included. The teams were great but not quite as close-knit. In the martial arts family, there would sometimes be ten of us going out to a bar or to Chi-Chi's for Mexican food. A lot of camaraderie was built eating and traveling together for tournaments.

One time, on a road trip to a competition, I was one of the drivers in our caravan. Something had happened with my car. We all drove into a gas station. This was when they were called "service stations," and they had a mechanic on site in an attached garage that repaired cars, while an attendant washed windshields and pumped your gas for you. I went in and asked the mechanic to look under the hood. Then he gave me his diagnosis. I went to discuss it with the others. Then Master Choi walked over. "What's going on here?"

Some of the students explained the problem with my car. They mentioned that we didn't know whether to believe this guy. Master Choi started over to confront him. Master Choi was angry because he thought they were trying to take advantage of me and he was going over to kick ass.

"No, no, no, sir!" they said, intervening and trying to calm him down. I clarified that it was something the mechanic thought the car might need.

"Oh, okay," Master Choi said, suddenly very calm.

But his defense of me was endearing. We were very fond of each other, and he told me several times that he considered me one of his daughters. In some ways he was a father figure to me. That they were all protective of me solidified that these were "my people."

Martial arts are different from any other kind of sport. It's an encompassing lifestyle. You don't go in there just to learn how to do kicks and punching or competing. There's much more to it. In the summer, our school held annual martial arts camps at Denison University for a week and trained together. It was fun, like attending band camp or something. All of these programs, done with the right attitude, demonstrated growth, contributed to our community, reinforced respect, and taught us how to effectively support each other, which created a cool atmosphere for everyone. We even shared holiday events and held award ceremonies to congratulate people for reaching new goals or excelling in some significant way. It was a highly unified community: we were multigenerational, multicultural, men, women, and children. At tournaments, we always had a whole entourage of people who came to cheer us on. It gave me such a good feeling and felt like being part of a family.

Meanwhile, I was enjoying the program at Ohio Dominican, so I stayed with it, planning to get my art degree there. Professor Mel strongly encouraged my artwork but especially abstract expression. I explored more conceptual artwork because it was expressive in a different kind of way. It came from a deeper, spiritual place within me that I had not investigated before. Working in abstracts seemed to connect me to the greater cosmos, a place beyond words. Some of what I created looked like something you might see beyond the stratosphere, out in the universe, or even beyond.

The college wasn't that far from my parents' house, and the martial arts school was so close, so I continued to live at home. My dad was still one of my main encouragers and supportive of my choices. I like to think he was happy with the developments in my artwork, and that I was doing good things and having fun while becoming a responsible adult. At school, I befriended a girl and we went to see concerts together like Billy Joel and Styx. Aside from that, campus was not my social gathering place. That was almost exclusively the domain of the martial arts community.

As students at a liberal arts college, we were required to take a certain number of religion or theology classes. I had begun asking a lot of questions. What I realized was that there's got to be more to this. For the time being, my attitude about religion class was, *Okay, I'm just going to get through this.* I had attended Catholic school from first grade all the way to college. It wasn't far from my thoughts that Catholicism represented all these rules. There were catechism classes, holy days, a list of dos . . . and mostly don'ts.

I went to church on Sundays, the sole representative of the Yee family. I felt it was my duty to be there saving our collective souls; I had to go there for everybody's sake. While attending St. Catharine's, I wanted to believe in something so badly, and I wanted to embrace the Catholic religion. But the more I learned, the more it stopped making sense to me. How can they talk about a loving God, then say if you don't go to confession for penance, you're condemned to hell? If you miss going to Mass, you're going to hell? That didn't seem right. I knew plenty of people who didn't attend church services. They seemed happy in their lives. There were other people whom I knew through martial arts—they weren't Catholic—and they appeared to be successful. Then, one of the sisters discussed different philosophers: St. Augustine, St. Thomas Aquinas, Socrates, and others. When she quoted Descartes—"I think, there for I am"—it opened my mind. I thought about that whole philosophy and remembered that this was something I had pondered as a seven-year-old kid. At that time, I was a little afraid I was the only person really existing in this reality. *In this consciousness that I exist in, does anything else truly exist? Does anyone else really exist? Unless I put myself in front of them, do I exist in their reality? What are the experiences of other people? What am I doing here? If a tree falls in the forest, and no one is around, does it make*

31

a sound? These thoughts were "unknown territory." I felt like I was the only person that thought this way. Because I didn't understand the ramifications of these alarming and terrifying thoughts, at that age, I used to cry at night. Since I had once pondered similar philosophies, when the Descartes line of thinking came up in college, it motivated me to learn more about different perspectives and how other people saw the world. It sparked my interest in a different kind of spirituality. I had a paradigm shift away from organized religion into more esoteric, New Age, and what some call "woo-woo" stuff. I felt some sense of connection to that reality. Taking the Bible literally didn't have as much meaning for me.

On campus, I was on my way somewhere and had to use the restroom. I detoured through the big bookstore and, all of a sudden, something stopped me in my tracks. On an endcap was a book called *Many Lives, Many Masters* by Brian Weiss, a psychologist known for hypnotizing people to regress them to their past lives. I started reading and thought, *Whoa! This is pretty interesting!* Then I read *The Celestine Prophecy* by James Redfield, the Seth books by Jane Roberts, and learned about channeling, Abraham Hicks . . . you name it. I was familiar with meditation to some degree through martial arts training. Between that and the books I was reading, I started my transformation from religion to a more spiritually based practice. There was a slew of information out there that resonated with me about my existence here, more so than the religion of my upbringing.

I still believe there's a higher power, a divine and infinite source. What I take away from all that I've read is that what you think or focus on is what you draw to yourself. It's all based on the law of attraction. What you experience is a result of the thoughts you think. Many motivational and inspirational speakers also believe this. It isn't new stuff. Albert Einstein said, "Everything is energy." Later I would learn Qigong and the Tai Chi practices that strengthen the Chi energy field in the body and engage your mind to focus and build vitality.

Reading about different philosophies began opening my mind to a lot of possibilities instead of the narrow track of religion. I just added this new learning to my already overloaded schedule. I really was my own Tiger Mom, the formidable Asian mother constantly pushing myself to achieve higher and higher levels of success. Even though I had already accomplished a lot in just a few years, I rarely took a break. My high energy levels made it easy to do a thousand kicks, train for days on end, and just keep going. Because I enjoyed everything that I was doing, up until an invitation to spend the summer in Florida, there seemed no reason to stop. College would be finished soon and that would be one less thing to worry about.

I took a full course load each year and my education seemed very important to my dad. A few years into it, he came into my bedroom. I could tell he'd been crying.

"I want you to make a promise that you will finish college," he said.

"Okay. I plan on it."

Something had happened that had brought this up in him. I didn't know what it was, and I never found out. I made the promise and filed it away. At the time, happy as I was, martial arts was the catalyst that had already begun a profound change and awakened new things in me. I didn't realize that this was just the tip of the iceberg and the ride was just beginning.

Great-grandfather Jin Jang Yee

Grandfather George Yee circa 1940

Grandmother Ying Ma Yee

(L to R) Brother Bob, Dad, brother Tom, and me

*My parents Nora Lai Yuk and
Peter Sum Fee Yee*

My brother Henry and me

Five-year-old Helen

High school graduation with Mom and Dad

Far East Restaurant circa 1940s

Yee's Restaurant circa 1970

March on Washington for gay and lesbian rights, 1987

Chapter 6

Fighting, No Fighting & Point Fighting

"Use only that which works,
and take it from any place you can find it."
~ Bruce Lee

Once I acquired the self-defense skills, I didn't feel the need to fight anymore. It was like my energy shifted. It occurred to me that my former energy may have been attracting negative people, those who bullied and made racist remarks. As I progressed, racist events occurred less frequently, and I stopped attracting bullies. As my role model Bruce Lee once said, "The best fight is no fight."

At one of the largest tournaments near Washington, DC, I participated in my very first competition as a yellow belt, the beginner's level. I mostly wanted to see what it was about. My focus then was all about *kata* forms and breaking bricks and boards. *Katas* are a series of linear blocks, punches, and kicks that create different patterns for fighting single or multiple opponents. They train muscle memory and condition thinking. *Katas* are more for showmanship: the way that you execute a kick shows your technique and precision. If your moves are sloppy, you won't get very high grades. I made sure my kicks, punches, and flow of my techniques were very fluid and sharp because those were the measurements of their scoring system. At that time, I wasn't interested in fighting at all and avoided it because it was not something I felt I was naturally good at.

At the DC tournament, I was super nervous, competing against twenty other people. Whether I succeeded or failed rested solely on me. If I messed up on a form, I couldn't blame anyone but myself. This was really a singular kind of achievement. Even with fighting, you're basically fighting on your own. All the pressure is on you as well as the accolades. And I won the silver, which not only felt pretty great, but was made all the more fantastic by being awarded the first trophy I had ever received!

Afterwards, about thirty of us stayed over a few extra days and did a tour of all the DC monuments. It was meaningful to me being surrounded by people I liked to be with. We just laughed and joked and had so much fun together.

One of the things I always loved to challenge myself with was going to open tournaments where all martial art systems are used, not Taekwondo exclusively. The Taekwondo moves I learned contained lots of power but initially weren't as graceful as Kung Fu moves. What I admired about the Kung Fu systems were the flowing, circular movements that were more elegant, more dancelike. However, as I ranked higher—dark blue and black belt levels—I enjoyed Taekwondo *katas* more because they became fancier and more graceful. As Taekwondo forms are very limited and short—about two minutes—at tournaments I'd watch the forms of the competition. If they ran four or five minutes long, I realized I wouldn't do well with just a two-minute form. Instead, I combined several Taekwondo forms. They didn't know I was blending two or three forms together, which helped my score. It was very affirming to be one of several people who always brought home a medal or trophy from every tournament. Winning became addictive, and I soon collected fifty trophies!

To be promoted to the next level in Taekwondo, you're not just learning a series of *katas* for each rank. You learn techniques, such as kicking and blocking, fighting skills, and self-defense skills, but Master Choi required an integration of these various disciplines. There's a whole system and philosophy to learn. At each new belt color or degree, there were certain obligations we were required to meet. I had to be able to give of my time, my self, and stay committed. It was required, on my way to earning a red or other intermediate belt, to teach some classes to lower-ranked students. Sometimes I taught kids' classes, which helped me learn how to pass on the knowledge I had attained. Each time I tested for a higher black belt ranking, one day of fasting was added to the original three. Along with other martial arts students seeking various black belt levels, I learned to meditate for twelve consecutive hours. At these intervals, we wrote essays about our martial arts journeys, including the changes we experienced in ourselves and the growth we had achieved. On testing day, we were asked, "What other things have you done?"

One of my best friends was Sunny, a well-rounded martial artist, both a very good fighter and forms competitor. She was part of the Amateur Athletic Union (AAU) that ran the show when I was competing. AAU later became the United States Taekwondo Union (USTU). Sunny competed all over the world; she was like a mentor to me, and I looked up to her. One night after sparring class, she said to me, "You know, Helen, if you didn't play around so much you could be a really good fighter."

Later that night, I gave her comment some real thought. Because she was a good judge of character and ability, I took her words seriously. She had no reason to tell me something unless it was true. Then I had an epiphany. What could I become if I really gave it my best effort? How would it affect my life? *Okay, I'm going to really buckle down and learn how to do some fighting!*

Point fighting was not as intimidating as full contact because one has to hold back punches and kicks. It is more of a tag game to get points with light contact. Unlike *katas* where the focus is on precision and form, in point tournament fighting you try to gain points to outscore your opponent. This kind of fighting is about timing and seeing an opening for attack, similar to the strategy of playing chess. I try to anticipate my opponent's next move and maybe draw them into a certain move that benefits my score. For example, I might do a roundhouse kick to my right side and leave myself open, so they do what I expect. Once they do, I counter with a spin back kick and move in with a technique that gives me a point.

Then there's full-contact fighting, the closest to being in a real fight. You've got all this gear on, but in order to win, both competitors are literally fighting as hard as they can and trying to knock each other out. I wasn't quite ready for that. However, I had learned quite a lot under Master Choi and felt empowered and very confident. That was enough for me. I didn't go looking for trouble or try to pick fights with anyone. I knew that if something came up, I could hold my own. It was a good feeling.

While still living at home, I was asleep in bed one night. My mom came to my room and woke me up.

"Helen, you need to go and get your dad."

"What's going on?" I asked. The restaurant was closed, and he was still there.

"There's two men in a car, and it looks like they're waiting for him to leave. They're sitting with their lights on in front of the restaurant."

I grabbed my nunchucks, threw them on the dashboard of my car, and drove over to the restaurant. Yee's had been robbed several times before. Who knows? Maybe they were scouting the place or planning to rob it that night too. When I got close, I saw a car idling with its parking lights on. It was the only other car in the parking lot besides Dad's. He was watching through the door. I gunned the engine and roared into the parking lot. I screeched my tires and skidded to a stop. My dad saw that it was me and opened the restaurant door.

"Come on, Dad, let's go!"

I kept an eye on the other car to make sure no one was getting out or coming toward us. They weren't. They didn't know who else was in my car with me, but they noticed the nunchucks. Dad got in his car, and we left. Already, martial arts was changing my life for the better.

With all the time I spent with the martial arts crowd attending all the competitions, and going to work and college, I barely had a social life. Outside of that, I had dated a few guys here and there. While it was fun, I found them mundane and predictable, and I didn't take any of them seriously. I had my own money and wasn't impressed by guys spending money on me for meals. As a result, these young men really didn't hold my interest.

One of my friends, whom I will refer to as Kristy, had gone to Florida to take care of her grandmother who had been in poor health. She and I had gotten to know each other pretty well, and she invited me to come down and stay with her for the summer. I gave it serious consideration. This Tiger Mom had been cracking the whip pretty much nonstop, and I was feeling a little exhausted. I had one semester left before graduation, and as luck would have it, my next competition was the national tournament happening in Florida at just the right time. I happily accepted Kristy's invitation. During training, I looked forward to having the summer off as soon as the national tournament finished. Summer sunshine, sand, palm trees, and beaches sounded like the ideal getaway! I could use a few umbrella drinks and a nice break from my super-hectic life. Then in the fall, I would return to Columbus and pick up right where I left off.

I was about to learn that life doesn't always go according to plan.

Chapter 7

Happy. Curious. Awakened.

"Size matters not. Look at me. Judge me by my size, do you?"
~ Yoda

In 1981, after successfully competing in point fighting, I had been training very enthusiastically for my first full-contact national competition. I drove down to Fort Myers, Florida the day before the National Martial Arts Competition excited, but also really nervous. After getting my feet wet with point fighting, I had finally committed to full-contact fighting. In point fighting, there were far more rules, and tapping your adversary somewhere on their body or head was the slight movement necessary to get the point. If I were to kick someone too hard in the head in point fighting, I would be disqualified. In a full-contact match, that could well be my intent. At this level, we didn't limit the power of our kicks and punches—we were going all out. This meant feeling the full force of every kick and punch with the intent of getting a technical knockout or knocking the opponent out. I was to experience my very first full-contact fight at the Nationals, and it felt as scary as sticking my head in a lion's mouth.

Once the team and I got to Florida, we had to weigh in, as always, then we went to get something to eat. As much as I wanted to stay up late and see the sights, getting a good night's rest is important for focus and stamina. Besides, I'd be seeing Kristy soon and there would be all summer to check out the area.

At that time, there weren't many women competing and particularly few in our weight division. As the underdog, no one expected a lot from me. My strongest feeling was that I just wanted to get it over with. Because I had no ranking, I was scheduled to fight nearer to the end of the championship, which meant carrying that feeling of butterflies in my stomach the whole day. Master Choi wanted me to fight as a black belt, and I was given one to compete at this level. My competitor was a woman who had gone to the same martial arts school I had. She was my senior, a second-degree black belt, and we were in the same flyweight division. She started with an apology.

"I'm sorry, Helen."

I took it to mean that she wasn't going to pull any punches and that she intended to win. "It's okay," I said.

With this being my very first match as a full-contact fighter, I certainly had no high expectations of my ability in this new arena. Master Choi and I agreed this would be a great opportunity to experience what full-contact fighting was like. While I didn't know how much I'd get hurt, I wasn't looking forward to being knocked out, even though it was a given that she would win. To say I was nervous would be an understatement. Waiting all day to fight was worse than the actual fight. The combination of having dry mouth, sweaty palms, and actually feeling dizzy added to my total self-doubt. My self-talk wasn't so great either at the time. For instance, *What the hell am I doing?* and *Who thought this was a good idea?* Once my name was called and after waiting so long, I was actually able to control the butterflies in my stomach and nerves. I was able to focus myself to do what my body was trained to do.

It's possible that Master Choi had known something I didn't. I won the match and placed second overall winning a silver medal! My opponent was visibly upset. I felt bad for her and even apologized to her. I later learned she'd lost weight, under the direction of Master Choi, to fight in that weight category.

As I think back I was never knocked out during a competition, but I did come close when I was training with my teammates. Master Choi demonstrated a combination kick and I foolishly leaned forward. Who would lean forward into a combination kick? My face ended up meeting his left foot! The lesson here is: Don't block with your face!

At the end of the tournament, I was thrilled to have won and equally excited to have a whole summer off to recoup and do as I liked. I said, "See ya later," to my teammates. I promised to catch up with them when I got back to Columbus in the fall. On the way to the place where Kristy was staying with her aunt, I felt pretty proud of myself for winning a silver at my very first full-contact fighting match! Maybe I had a future as a full-contact fighter after all! Sunny's pivotal words to me, that I could be a really good fighter if I stopped playing around, were already proving to be right. What could this lead to?

When I finally got to Kristy's, after introductions to her aunt and brother, we had a celebratory drink and got high. As the stress I'd been carrying melted away, I began to feel extremely wiped out. "I know I just got here, but I really need to take a nap," I said.

Kristy happily showed me where I could crash, and in moments, I was totally gone. Later, I woke up, feeling very much refreshed. I went out to where she and her aunt were sitting. "You literally slept for twenty-four hours," Kristy said.

"Are you kidding me?"

One whole day went by, and I had missed it! That was bizarre for me, having never done that before, but I had never been so exhausted. After that, we got right into having some fun. I was fully rested, wide awake, and ready to go—and hungry!

Kristy offered to make me something to eat or to go out to eat, my choice. I wanted to get an idea of what was around and see more of the area. We hopped in her car and took off.

The west coast of Florida was gorgeous. Spanish moss dangled from live oaks, palm trees swayed in the warm, salty breeze, white sand beckoned, and emerald waters sparkled in blazing sunlight. What was not to like? I was on my own, nearly twelve hundred miles from home. And while I wasn't trying to get away from my parents and responsibilities, it felt great to have a break from the back-to-back activities I had imposed on myself. At twenty-one, I was making my own decisions, and this felt like a good one. A whole new world of options opened up. I sensed a freedom I had never felt before. All day open with nowhere I had to be. All around me, people were operating at a slower pace, and it took a bit of getting used to. What I liked about it was the feeling of being on vacation with plenty of time. No one was in a hurry, and I relaxed into the calmer cycle of the South.

Along with the exterior changes in scenery, I had been going through a series of significant internal spiritual changes. Over time, I hadn't done much with the whole Catholic thing. By the time I got to Florida, I stopped altogether. Instead of going to church on Sunday, I slept late, and later we'd go to the beach. The beach was my church. I felt connected to the "All That Is" in the ocean more than in a religious building. Because I had no commitments, my thoughts drifted to other things like feeding my soul, partying, and having fun. It was like Spring Break only better because I had a whole summer. Kristy and I ended up having drinks, getting high, and going to the beach every day. I was starting to feel a deep connection with the sand and the sea. Kristy and I got along really well. Even better than I expected. We went to a lot of different places and talked about everything. It was nice being the center of attention and having someone to talk to every day who seemed to understand me and liked me for who I was. I felt I could be myself and, for the first time, I experienced real contentment without the need to perform.

That summer seemed to fly by. In August, I realized my time there would soon be ending. I thought about going back to finish my last semester, but we were having such a good time, a part of me really wanted to stay. I wanted to understand that feeling. Was it because it was a new place? Because I didn't have to work? Because of the company I was keeping? I recognized that sometimes I felt strongly attracted to Kristy but I brushed those feelings aside. I wasn't sure what I was feeling but it was different and I didn't want to take a chance of ruining our friendship, because we had a lot of fun! We had similar interests in music, martial arts, going to concerts and having out at the beach. We laughed a lot. I was still dating guys, and she was too. At the time, I didn't know she had a crush on me, and that we had feelings for each other, her more than me.

Then, something intimate happened between us. We were both like, "Oh my gosh, what is this? I didn't expect this to happen." I didn't know what to do. We did not recognize or acknowledge that we were gay. We had no gay friends. At least we didn't think so.

But I also felt, *Wow this is great!* Inside I was happy, curious, and awakened. The relationship with Kristy was very different from being with guys. For me, men were easy to figure out. I knew when I was in a relationship with a guy that I called the shots. And if they didn't like it, I didn't care. Okay, so what? We're done. Their feelings really didn't touch me, and it never bothered me. This relationship was different and complex. We communicated deeper feelings and emotions. It was easier to connect with her because I could really get into the emotional feeling of the conversation, whereas with guys, they're generally not feely or emotional. That experience with Kristy was reorienting.

Now I had a major dilemma. I was supposed to be back in Columbus soon to complete my last semester and graduate. I promised my dad that I would finish. What was I going to do about the promise? What did this new information mean to my life? Should I count that romantic interlude as a one-time thing or accept that this happened and follow the path to see where it might lead? Could I move to Florida, stay with Kristy, and make this relationship work? I felt this incredible draw to stay with Kristy because this was my first lesbian relationship . . . and I was in love with her. It felt right, and she wanted me to stay. Maybe I wanted to stay partly because I was just tired and needed the break from everything to last a little longer.

Before this happened with Kristy, I didn't know that was me. She and I never admitted that we were gay. We were just in love.

Even when I came out to my best friend in Ohio—which was a very big thing—my explanation seemed to confuse her. "I fell in love with someone who is the same sex as me," I said simply. Barb was very gracious, and didn't know anyone who was gay, but she had one question.

"Have you ever had those feelings about me?"

"No, it doesn't work that way."

I always thought it was God's joke, because here I was, finally feeling comfortable in my own skin and being Chinese. Then He throws this curve ball. "So, how about this . . . You're gay!"

"Ahhh . . . okay."

It took a while for the reality of the idea to really sink in, to saturate the fabric of my daily life, and make its full weight felt. Finally, the realization hit me like a kick to the chest. This is a game changer. *Wow, I'm gay.*

With this epiphany, I looked at all those old experiences through a new lens. So, this was why I had had crushes on female coaches or teachers and why I was attracted to some of my female classmates and friends. Those thoughts led me to my own revelations about why I never felt right dating guys, and why I felt like I was playing a role, like I was acting. It explained why dating experiences with guys left me feeling awkward and thinking that there had to be more to it than this.

The incident with Kristy began to solidify my new sexual orientation. What now? How do I move forward from here? How much was I going to be bullied and ostracized for this?

I quickly learned the difference between being Chinese and being a lesbian. You can't hide being Chinese, but you can hide being gay. Living in Florida, I could stall telling family and friends until I wanted to reveal that part of myself to them—if ever. By then, I would have figured out more pressing issues in my life, like who I was, how I wanted to live my life, and finding the right job.

Being with Kristy was exciting and new but it was still precarious navigating the relationship in an 80s anti-gay Deep South. There's a lot you have to hide about your life when you're a lesbian. However, it's much like any other out-of-bounds relationship. Although there were a few people who were compassionate, we were careful about what we mentioned "in passing" so it didn't open up a can of worms we really didn't want to talk about. Our conversations around others were guarded to protect us from being exposed to the opinions of people who didn't agree with our lifestyle choices. This meant I didn't talk about which of us hogs the blankets or the bed. I didn't publicly complain that while we were making out in the car one time, some stranger tapped on the window and said, "We aren't having any of that here." We counted ourselves lucky that it ended there, and that the stranger walked away. Others had not been as fortunate. So, just like people who keep secrets about their extramarital affairs, we kept our private lives mostly to ourselves and downplayed where and when it was necessary.

In the meantime, I had the freedom to pursue happiness in my own way. The first thing I had to acknowledge was how this would affect college and my living arrangements. It meant postponing my last semester. I thought I could manage telling my parents about my decision without "coming out" as gay. I wanted to hold off on that for now. I felt confident that I could play it cool and not give myself away. The whole drive back to Columbus, I rehearsed what I'd say to each of them. I don't remember if I put myself in their shoes, imagining what I would sound like when I explained why I was postponing that final semester. I just knew I had to do it and get it behind me. I strengthened my resolve with thoughts of being in love, going to the beach, how magical nature was there, and how exciting and different my new life would be. The sooner I accomplished this mission, the sooner I could get back to that new, thrilling life with Kristy.

At my parent's house, I thought it would be best to talk to them separately. I first talked to Mom.

"Mom, I'm not going back to school just yet. I'm going back to Florida."

"Oh . . . . Wow," she said, then got very quiet. But she was always quiet. Telling her was the easy part. I couldn't read her. Maybe she was disappointed. Maybe she was sad her only daughter was suddenly moving so far away. She didn't show much emotion, but then, I hadn't promised her that I would finish. One parent down, one to go.

I wasn't one to make snap decisions. Because this decision would affect my dad, I knew telling him was going to be really hard. I didn't want to get into an argument. I was careful in the phrasing of my decision so that he wouldn't try to convince me to stay in Columbus. I had given it a lot of thought. I expected him to be disappointed and unhappy about it because he's always wanted at least one of his kids to finish college and get a degree. What that stemmed from was never shared with me. Maybe because I would have been the first in our family, in generations, to do so. I completely underestimated the importance of this promise.

I was nervous about telling him, especially with having only one semester to go. But I had to do this, difficult as it was, so that I could go on with my life in the way that seemed best to me at the time. The sooner I got it over with, the sooner I could hit the road. I just wanted to go back to Florida. Out of respect, I sat down with him.

"Dad, I made a decision to go back to Florida and not finish my last semester at this time."

Then I waited, while he absorbed the gravity of those words. I expected him to ask questions. I thought he would make some suggestions, like he had at the pool when he was teaching me how to become a better diver. There was a chance that I was making too much of it, and he wouldn't take it as hard as I imagined he might. I was banking on my statement leaving him little room to argue.

He didn't argue. He didn't go off on a yelling tirade. He didn't scream or anything. But he wouldn't even look at me. He was stunned. That didn't last very long. "Just go!" he said emphatically. "JUST GO!"

Whoa! Now I was stunned. That really hurt. No more discussion. It was over. He just wanted me out. The tension was so thick and the energy had turned so heavy in the house, I decided to pack my stuff and leave that very day.

My father and I are a lot alike in that our love runs deep, however, our words are few. Of one thing I am certain: our love for each other was never in question. Although we did not understand each other at this point in time, I always loved my father and I knew he loved me. What neither of us could have ever known is that this would be the last conversation we'd ever have. Though I can't honestly say I'd do it differently if I had to do it again, I will say that I wish he could see me now. He'd be smiling and realize I graduated from university and I am living "THE" American dream he'd wished for me.

Chapter 8

Wild Sea Animals

I don't remember if my dad had ever been that angry with me—or anyone else—ever before. I wasn't sure if he was angry about my dropping out of college, or if he knew that I was gay. I don't know how he could have known. It's possible he figured out I wanted to go back to Florida because of my girlfriend; that would have been more devastating to him than my not finishing college. After that, I didn't call home or keep in contact with my family, except to share my new address and phone number. I just didn't feel close to them, and I hadn't for a long time. My mom maintained the slenderest thread of communication—just wanting to know where I was—but rarely called. Even though it bothered me deeply that things had gone badly with Dad, I've never been one to dwell on the negative. Without their physical presence, it was easy to shift my attention to having a bright future.

I was in my twenties! I was in love and having adventures and living my life. By the time I got back to my beautiful surroundings and my girlfriend, the whole incident with Dad had been pushed mostly out of my mind. Kristy's grandmother passed away after years of being bedridden, which freed us up to move wherever we wanted. Now that I was officially on my own, I focused on having fun and being in the moment.

I believed I could still get a good job with my artistic talent. Pretty soon, a graphic design company hired me. At first it was great being an artist and getting paid to use my talents. I was living on my own, paying my own bills, and feeling very grown up. After being a graphic designer for a while, the idea of it began to lose its luster. Most of the work entailed producing other people's ideas, which wasn't as creative as I had imagined it would be. And on top of that, I'd just spent three and a half years of my life training for this job, only to discover I hated it. I began realizing I still had a lot to figure out about myself and what to do with my life. What did I like to do? If I could work at anything, what would it be?

I shifted into doing odd jobs for a while, which let me explore other ways of earning income. My default was restaurant work since I could do it in my sleep. It was an okay interim job that held me over while I looked for other work I enjoyed more. I was an expediter at a fancy seafood restaurant on the water. Then I moved on to a building material supply store. I was very good as a cashier and got promoted quickly. Then they asked me to work in the paint department. So, I did that.

One of the things they sold there was palm tree cutting tools. In Florida, dead palm fronds are unattractive and a real nuisance. I thought doing that would be kind of cool! My very first taste of being an entrepreneur began when I started a palm tree cutting service. Using my graphic design knowledge, I made fliers about my new business, and I passed them out door-to-door in retirement communities. I connected with some of the regulars at the building supply store and handed flyers out there too. I made a lot of friends with older people, all seniors, who were probably a little lonely. They'd call me, and I'd cut down their palm branches. I set my own hours and worked when I wanted to. After freshening the look of their palm trees, they often invited me into their homes for lunch or dinner, and even to swim in their pool. I loved working outside, making money, and meeting all kinds of new people. I felt I was living an enviable life in paradise. I lived with Kristy in three places on Florida's gulf side: Port Charlotte, Punta Gorda, and Boca Grande. We went to the beach and got high almost every day and did life pretty much like any other typical couple who lived together in the 80s.

What I loved about Florida wasn't just the new discoveries about myself and the freedom to be me—there was the magnificent beauty of nature. On my first visit to the beach, I hesitated to swim in the water. The sea was so enormous and there were many scary stories about the deep. But as I became more comfortable, my fear turned to awe. Of the years I lived in Florida, my favorite memories were of going to Boca Grande beach early in the day, before any crowds appeared. It was a hidden treasure then, known only to the locals. We'd park the car on the side of the road, grab our Igloo cooler and a blanket, and hike through tall, grassy dunes. Finally, we'd make our way onto soft, white sand with hardly a soul in sight. Our own personal heaven.

Each day I became more comfortable with the ocean. Slowly, I became familiar with the sea life that lived there. I was astonished to see the brilliant creatures that survived in the crevices of beautiful mini-islands of coral when swimming out to the sandbar. My favorite thing was snorkeling because, unlike diving which required expensive gear, you could put on your weight belt, mask, and fins and just swim out. We were snorkelers. Swimming underwater was so surreal, it was like another world. We'd see barracuda and huge manatees. Occasionally, I saw sea urchins, colorful starfish (including watermelon starfish), and live sand dollars, which were green, not like the white-bleached ones in seashell stores or souvenir shops. I swam by a small eel as well as stingrays. Anytime I saw puffer fish around, I took my diver's knife and jokingly wiggled it in front of them. They responded by puffing up in a spiky warning. Despite that, they're cute as can be. Flounder quickly burrowed themselves under sand when they saw me coming toward them. Every day brought a spectacular adventure of beauty, and every time I encountered these wonderful creatures I was amazed. It was a special blessing to look out and see schools of dolphins playing in the water. They'd launch up into the air, skin gleaming and water droplets cascading like diamonds, as they flipped and did their own happy dance! When the enormous manatees slowly paddled into the area, it was magical to be in their presence. Both manatees and dolphins would swim right up to us. The feeling of communing and being trusted by wild sea animals left me in awe.

After swimming and exploring, I'd return to the beach. I'd lay out on a blanket to soak in the sun's heat, allowing the rays to dry and bronze my skin. This was more relaxing than anything I could imagine.

For me, the water has always been a place of serenity and calm—transcendent. The inviting warmth of the sun along with the lapping ocean begged me to come in, stay near, and play all day. On those days, I'd be lost in timelessness until the sun dipped into the western horizon and it would be time to go. Spending days at Boca Grande was my nirvana.

Another time, we went up to what the locals called the phosphate docks. We walked from the beach at Boca Grande, and then we jumped off the docks into the water. When you're there in the water at night, your body literally glows this weird green. "What the heck is this? What's going on?" I asked. And it's not because we were high, it was because of the high concentration of phosphates in the water from mining and shipping. There were lots of other unusual things we checked out, like shark bypass bridge. For thrills, we used to jump off into the deep water below without a care in the world. One day someone driving on the bridge stopped their vehicle and called out to us. "Hey you guys! Do you know this is a shark bypass?"

I don't even know what we said to them. We were probably stoned and just fooling around. We were in our twenties and had our whole lives ahead of us. We thought we were invincible and going to live forever. Never mind that most of the country was a little shark-phobic after watching *Jaws* not many years before, a movie in which a shark attacked unsuspecting beach goers. I had heard that shark skin feels like sandpaper. I remember one time jumping in the water there and feeling something rub against my leg that was rough and sandpapery. I'm sure that was a shark. Some people might say I'm lucky to still have both legs. I don't know how I even survived that or my years down there.

Part of our adventures included having bonfires on the beach and getting high. We once watched as three funnel clouds stretched their ominous, pointy fingers from a treacherous-looking sky to touch the ocean and then pulled back up. Such a powerful sight. We should have been running for cover, yet it was so amazing and beautiful to see the force of nature, we just stayed there watching it all. Maybe we couldn't move because we were so fricking high!

Another time we went snorkeling and were just having a good time. Overhead the clouds were black, but we were too naïve to care. We believed we were indestructible. And maybe we thought under the water we were safe enough. I remember swimming around, looking down. Suddenly everything in the ocean lit up like Super Bowl stadium lights. We surfaced at the same time and just looked at each other. "What the hell? We better get out of the water!"

We found out later that a bolt of lightning hit the water a distance away, and it lit up the sea! It's the kind of stuff you never hear anyone talk about (but we were lucky enough to live through it.) We didn't even know this stuff could happen!

One other incredible event happened when Kristy and I were around the sandbar. We were enjoying our day, swimming and exploring like we had dozens of times before. We decided to swim back. For whatever reason, Kristy didn't have her snorkel mask on. Luckily, I did. We had swum right smack into a school of jellyfish! "You better get your mask on," I said, "because these jellyfish are huge!"

And they were! I had never seen anything like it; they were at least four feet in diameter. They surrounded us, and some were bigger than my body! Since they travel very slowly, we swam underwater where we could see them and maneuvered our bodies around them. But I did look right into the middle of one of the big ones and saw the stinging filament. It was mesmerizing watching them open and close their bells to swim. So graceful, I'll never forget it.

After getting into the water one season at Boca Grande, we found massive amounts of perfect whelks—the kind you'd see in a shell factory—lying all over the floor of the ocean. They even had living things inside them. I don't know how they happened to be there or where they came from. That was just one of many incredible sightings. Even if you went out to the beach every day, you could never be sure what might be waiting for you. But if you went to the same place every day, you would see the same little eel that hid in a crevice, and the same sea urchin on the other side, and the same school of fish that swim there because it was their neighborhood.

One downside of living in Florida was being unable to find the kind of martial arts school I really wanted to be a part of. I practiced my own blend of spirituality, and, as long as we weren't overtly affectionate in public, we didn't catch too much flak from people, and no one interfered with us. But there was one instance when we were living in Fort Myers. Kristy and I were at The Shell Factory. Some guy was with a few of his friends and made a comment towards me that I did not like. Kristy knew him, but he hadn't made the comment to her. He was just being a bully, but I didn't have to take that crap anymore. I got right in his face. "Do you want to take this outside?" I asked.

Suddenly everything shifted, and he was trying to get away from me. I was basically waiting to see what he would do next. As soon as he moved, I did this quick, powerful shove right to his chest. I knew it would knock him completely off balance if he wasn't expecting it. And he wasn't. In the midst of display shelves filled with fragile shells everywhere, he started falling backwards. I was like, "Oh, shoot!" For a second it looked like he was going to fall into one of them. Luckily for him, he landed on the floor. He had totally underestimated me, and now he was humiliated in front of all his friends. I walked away thinking even though I hadn't been in a martial arts school in a while, my reflexes were still as sharp as ever.

My life in Florida never felt boring or mundane. There was always some new thing to explore, somewhere else exciting to go, or a marvel of nature that would reveal itself to me. One of the most unique experiences of my life happened while I thought I was asleep. While Kristy and I were sleeping in bed, I suddenly became aware of the fact that I could feel my eyelids. They were shut, but I could see the whole room through them. I looked over and saw my girlfriend's body lying in bed. It kind of freaked me out. *Okay, this is really weird!* I tried to say her name. Nothing. I tried to call out, but nothing came out of my mouth. *Holy crap! What is going on?* I tried to yell. I tried to scream. I tried to call out to her, but not one sound came out.

Oh my God, this isn't right! Something doesn't feel right. I can't stay like this! I wanted to sit up, and I sensed that I had. I hadn't yet realized what was happening. I turned to step onto the floor. As I did that, my being sank into the floor and then shot up to the ceiling. From the ceiling I looked around the room, then I saw my body lying there, in the bed next to my girlfriend. When I sat up, only my spirit being had done so, not my physical body! Next, I decided to go into the kitchen. I just floated there. But from this height I saw a cup with all my paintbrushes in it on top of our refrigerator. I didn't think anything about that but did notice how vivid everything was. I couldn't get over how real it all felt. I wasn't even thinking about my being out of my body, except that I saw myself. When I realized I was out of my body, I thought I was dead and panicked. *Oh my God, what is happening?* I thought. *AHHH!* As soon as I started freaking out, boom! I slammed right back into my body.

The next morning, I woke up wondering if what had happened was real. I had read about astral projection, but I didn't know how to do that. Then, I remembered seeing the cup on top of the refrigerator which was weird because I was missing my paintbrushes. I had looked for them everywhere because I wanted to paint sand dollars which I would later sell. When I couldn't find the brushes, I thought I must have lost them or thrown them out with the trash. When I remembered having seen them during my out-of-body experience, I had to go check out whether the brushes were on the refrigerator or not. Then I would know if I had actually left my body. I got a chair, stood on it and looked on top of the fridge. Sure enough, my paintbrushes there! They were in a cup and shoved to the back of the refrigerator, just as I had seen them! I would never have known they were up there because I wasn't tall enough to see that high. My girlfriend must have put them up there and then forgotten to mention it to me.

That was such a unique phenomenon to me; I remember thinking, *What the hell was that?* My time in Florida was magical in so many ways. The relationship with my girlfriend was significant in that it allowed me to discover aspects of who I really am. We had a lot of fun together. But the next thing I knew, six years had passed. Even though I stayed with her, I had become unhappy. To make matters worse, I just didn't know how to get myself out of the relationship. I agonized for a long time about how to end it. Then my mother called.

"Helen, I have bad news about your dad."

Chapter 9

Gathering Dad's Spirit

Until that phone call, I had been like thousands of other twenty-somethings, expecting their parents to live into their seventies or beyond, or at least to the age of their own parents. My grandfather was in his eighties but still alive. I was so comfortable with that notion, that anything outside of that order didn't make sense. I rarely considered the inevitable fact that they were wearing down, or that their health issues and life in general were grinding away at their vitality. Certainly, we are never prepared for an untimely surprise.

"Your dad had a heart attack." I was blindsided to hear that it had taken his life. Initially, my mind could not comprehend that we were talking about my dad and not my grandfather who had sold the restaurant years before and retired to Vancouver, Canada to live with his daughter. My mother had not been any more prepared than I had. Whatever chance there had been of any future reconciliation between my father and I had disappeared in the breath of my mother's words. What would be forever lodged in my mind was the look of anger he had felt toward me and the unbearable weight of his disappointment. I tried to absorb the reality that I would never speak to him again, never see him alive again, never hear his voice or his laugh. This reality check shook me.

The guilt that rose up in me was like a dark, churning sea. I had not kept in touch with my family through phone calls, which in those days were billed by the minute. I had not returned for Chinese or American holidays, or birthdays, or reunions. The years in Florida had flown by, almost like one great, long summer vacation. My mind felt stuck in a weird time loop. This couldn't be happening. Tears poured from my eyes as I told my mom I would come home. Everyone would be there. I would probably have to explain myself—my abrupt departure and my long absence—which would be awkward. In Chinese culture, such send-offs are usually preceded by family gatherings and tearful goodbyes amidst a banquet of tasty dishes. I didn't know how my family had explained me to their friends, and I never asked. Despite all this, I wanted to be there for the funeral. It was the right thing to do. My mother needed me.

Even though my girlfriend didn't think it was a good idea for me to drive alone, a break from her would help me think. If she came with me, I would have to explain her. My . . . roommate? What would Kristy think of that? Would it hurt her feelings? I thought this was a less than ideal time to introduce her as my girlfriend/ partner/lover to everyone in Columbus—especially my family—when I wanted out of the relationship and was planning some kind of escape.

The 1,200-mile trip north was a blur. Even though I had lost my maternal grandmother, this wasn't the same. She had been distant, having never lived in the United States. She followed the Jewish faith tradition and was buried in China within twenty-four hours. Only recently did it come to light through a cousin that my maternal grandfather had two wives, one who bore his children and one who did not. In China at that time, it was not unusual for a man to have two wives. Photos had been sent to us of the mourners crying and wearing dark colors (in the Chinese tradition) as the plumes of smoke rose from burning joss paper—also known as ghost money—at the graveside to ensure safe passage of the deceased into the afterlife. I expected to see many of the same things at my father's funeral.

I mainly tried to wrap my mind around the fact that my father had died. Even though he had disowned me, in the back of my mind I always thought we would one day talk about it, that somehow it would be resolved. I thought I might consider changes that he would agree with, or I'd be able to explain myself to him and make him understand. At that age, I didn't really understand fully the idea of forever, or the permanence of certain decisions. It was surreal that someone I had lived with was gone. He died not knowing the real me. I struggled to accept that there would be a great many things about me and my life that my father would never know. Our window of time had closed.

Even though I had not been in contact with him in recent years, and that bothered me a lot, it was difficult to picture Mom without Dad, or the Cadillac without Dad driving it, or the restaurant without him working in it. Arriving in Columbus after being away for so long, our house looked smaller than I remembered, but it was a bustling hive of voices. Inside, there were people sitting in every room talking somberly and telling stories, discussing arrangements, speaking on the phone, and bringing dishes of food. No one smiled. Cousins stood with my older brothers who were there with their wives, all swollen-eyed and downcast. They all knew about the rift between me and my dad, but no one spoke of it. Could they tell by looking at me how much I had changed?

They were surprised to see me. My brother Henry hovered at the edge of the doorway like he wanted to escape. Everyone exchanged hellos. A sort of altar had been set up where Dad's picture stood prominently surrounded by food and smoldering incense. It was strange to be standing in our house with so many people and my father not among them. A part of my mind seemed to think that he would eventually show up because he always enjoyed these sorts of gatherings. The star of the show was conspicuously absent. At times, I thought I could hear his voice when my older brothers spoke. But I knew it was my mind playing tricks on me because I really could not imagine that he was truly gone. Maybe he was still at the restaurant . . . .

"Where's mom?" I asked.

But before anyone could answer, one of my aunties called out, "There's Helen!"

"Helen's here!" another chimed in. Women came out to greet me and then ushered me into the kitchen. Though my mother always appeared elegant and put together, and she was even now, I was surprised by how small and tired she looked. Aunts, related and unrelated, uncles, and my mother's closest friends swarmed around her at the dining room table. Mom seemed glad to see me. I went to her and hugged her. I felt my throat tighten and tears burned my eyes.

I sat down at the table with them just listening and feeling all that was going on around me. It seemed they were glad for someone new in the room, a distraction from the pain of current circumstances. No one asked about why I had left to go to Florida so unexpectedly when I had originally planned to return, or why I had not been in touch with anyone. In many ways, they were as careful as I was about what we talked about. But with so much grief, it was also easy to be quietly reflective and avoid problematic conversations. Everyone was preoccupied with their own thoughts and how their lives were affected by the loss of my father. My grandfather acknowledged me but was very quiet. He sipped his tea and stared out the window.

At the wake, the room was filled with flower arrangements sent from those expressing their condolences. The floral scent was cloying and overpowering. When I look back on that time, it's almost like watching a movie from someone else's life. I couldn't believe it was happening, yet every downcast face, every sad expression confirmed that it was real. I kept thinking of all the things I wished I had said to my dad. I was regretting my missed opportunities. I don't remember if I was concerned that his spirit would now begin to visit, or even haunt me, because of my broken promise. Certainly, such things had occurred in our extended family: a certain person becoming the target of restless ancestor spirits. For the sake of closure, and partly to prevent the possibility, I went up to the casket and looked at my dad. My sadness was so strong, words tumbled out of my mouth at the sight of him.

"Dad, I'm sorry. I'm sorry you didn't get to see me graduate. I promise I will come back and finish college. And I will help Mom." After sharing those heartfelt words, I wiped my eyes and tried to pull myself together. Although I sensed some measure of heaviness had lifted, the weight of the loss had not. The numbness had not.

The actual service was brief but well-attended and carried out with a mix of Catholic and Chinese traditions. During the funeral, I thought about all that I had learned from my dad. He had been my biggest encourager for many years. Even though I missed that, I had found more supporters. Of course, no one could or would ever replace my dad. He instilled in me several things that would carry me through life, that I would always credit him for. He taught me to have fun, and I had learned how to do that very well. Even though it had left him disappointed, I wondered if he realized it. Had he ever wished that he had handled our last meeting differently? Maybe in the spiritual realm, there was still time for me to reconcile with him and honor him for all that he brought to my life.

I sifted through the things I could have done differently. These thoughts didn't take me in a good direction. The past was done. I couldn't change it any more than I could change being Chinese. Instead, I decided to focus on better memories of my dad: his encouragements, the crazy little quirks that made him unique, and fun things we did when we were close. I remembered that my dad used to take me to this place called Grill & Skillet, a real old-school, cash-only diner. It was within walking distance of our house. We'd walk in, sit at the counter, and he would order two hamburgers for us. Sometimes we'd stay there and eat, and sometimes he'd get them to-go. They were old-fashioned, sizzling-hot burgers wrapped in paper. I don't know if it was being in his company, or the fact that it was an unexpected treat, but those burgers always tasted so good! I drove by that way and the Grill & Skillet is still there—and was packed! (It's still there as I write.)

The post-funeral caravan of cars traveled from the funeral home to Scioto Downs, which stood just south of the city, where my father had died. The procession made a big loop around the enormous parking lot. In Chinese tradition, this is to symbolically gather his spirit from the place where he spent his last hours. Next, we went to the section of the cemetery that is specifically dedicated to Chinese burials. My father would be laid to rest next to his grandfather's tombstone. Family members carried a picture of my father to the burial site and a special tray of food was left on the casket. It contained rice, a crispy kind of pork, oranges, and something to drink. Following the funeral ceremony, eating chicken is traditionally supposed to help the spirit of the deceased fly to heaven. Eating duck protects the spirit when it crosses the Three Rivers along the path to the afterlife. Finally, miniature objects like cars, houses, televisions, and other useful items for the afterlife are made of folded joss paper and burned. This is done so that the deceased can lead a lavish and a comfortable life, even after death.

After the graveyard service, a somber group of family and many friends gathered at the restaurant. People sat at tables and talked. Some told stories, a few funny ones, of how they met my dad, and other cherished memories. Our family sat together, and I sat near my mom and her friends who were trying to get her to eat. Many people came by and offered their condolences and kind words. The food on her plate sat untouched. She looked somehow stunned but deeply reflective, possibly remembering a conversation with him or an event where they both smiled in happier times. After the sale of the restaurant, they had hoped to live out their golden years together. My father had gone to the horse races one day and passed away there very unexpectedly. My dad and the restaurant had been her whole life. Now all she had was a house and my father's belongings. Even my brothers were drifting further away from her.

I knew then that I would move back, re-enroll in college, and get the promised degree. Even though my earthly relationship with Dad was complete, the one with my mother was still ongoing. As much as I could, I wanted to help and support her through this time. Maybe she and I would have a different, but better relationship.

At the end, as people began to leave, I stood with my mom as she passed out red envelopes and sweets. Red symbolizes happiness, and passing out the envelopes, which contain a single coin, signifies the end of the mourning period. The candy is to be ingested before returning to one's home to mark a fresh beginning. To carry it all the way home is to invite bad luck.

Experiencing the fragility of life for the first time, I saw how unexpected turns can happen in the blink of an eye. It forced me to finally address my relationship with Kristy. I secretly hoped that moving back to Columbus would give me an easy, plausible out. On the drive back to Boca Grande, I mentally rehearsed many break-up scenarios. The ideal situation in my mind would be if Kristy wanted to stay in Florida. I hoped that she was as ready as I was to end our relationship and move on. When it came right down to it, I guess I wanted her to dump me. I just knew it wasn't going to work out with us. I didn't even entertain moving both of us to Ohio. Maybe I wanted to be able to remember Florida as a special and magical time, its own chapter. Returning to Columbus would mean a lot of changes. My time would be allocated differently. No more days languishing on the beach, no more hours of swimming in the ocean. It meant finding a sustainable career path that I enjoyed, with the freedoms I experienced as an entrepreneur in Florida. First and foremost, it was time to keep the promise I had made to my dad. But until I could get a new job and a new place of my own, it meant staying with Mom temporarily. I wanted to be fair to myself about what living a gay lifestyle entailed in my hometown, and this meant figuring out who I could trust with that information. There was still a lot to think about.

My trip to Florida was barely more than a plan to pick up my things and say goodbye to Kristy. "You know I'm moving back to Columbus." I said. "I just came back to get my stuff."

"Then I will move there with you."

And why wouldn't she? She was happy. She didn't know I wanted out. I didn't feel I was being fair to move her back to Ohio and then break up with her. I wanted to be considerate of her feelings and break it off. But because I couldn't quite muster the courage or find the proper words to say, I was unable to break up at that time. She misread my unhappiness as being depressed about the death of my dad. I resigned myself to the fact that this was too complicated and that it wasn't the right time to end the relationship.

Kristy wasn't put off about having to stay with my mom until we could find our own place. We had lived in a similar way for a while with her aunt. On the brighter side, it was nice to have support through all the coming changes, but I felt like I was taking advantage of Kristy's feelings for me. How she reacted and felt mattered to me more than I ever imagined it would, and I didn't want to create an enemy or hurt her. But with each day that passed I knew we were increasingly incompatible. I also knew myself well enough to know that I could last under this dissatisfaction only so long, and I was curious about what else was out there. But until I figured it all out, Kristy and I packed our lives into cardboard cartons and returned the keys to the apartment. On moving day, we each drove north in separate vehicles filled with all our worldly possessions.

As Boca Grande disappeared in the rearview mirror, I wanted to remember all the amazing experiences I had had there. Although I was a little nervous about going back, I carried with me the knowledge that I had traveled far from home and had lived on my own terms for the last several years. I felt empowered in a new way, and I couldn't help wondering what the future would hold. I was edging toward a new kind of freedom; not caring what anyone thought about me. But I still had a lot to learn.

Chapter 10

Confidence Building

Once I got back to Columbus, I picked up almost where I'd left off. I went to work for a short time at Cochrane's Drug Store, Kristy and I moved in with Mom temporarily, and I returned to finish college at Ohio Dominican.

At Cochrane's, Zane, who was surprised to see me, hired me back on a temporary basis while I got settled into the old midwestern groove. While working one day, I happened to notice a particular magazine rack filled with *Playboy*, *Penthouse*, and other magazines. When I noticed the name Larry Flynt on the cover of *Hustler*, an old memory came flooding back. When I was about thirteen, my family and I were living in our new house. It was a relatively safe neighborhood given the times. I often rode my bike past the Columbus School for Girls (CSG) on Broad Street, which wasn't far, and across the street into Bexley near Jeffrey Mansion and the city swimming pool. Sometimes I went swimming there. One day, our home phone rang. Although I don't remember the conversation word-for-word, it went something like this:

"Hello?"

"Hello, this is Larry Flynt. Is Helen there?"

"Speaking."

"Helen, I'm a magazine publisher, and I've seen you around the neighborhood. I'd like to take some pictures of you."

I didn't know that name and was even more clueless about the magazine he published. What I initially thought was, *Oh wow, this is kind of cool!* At some point during his introduction, I heard the word pornography, a word I had never heard before that day.

"What is that?" I asked.

"You know, photographing you without your clothes."

Suddenly, I felt swallowed by an enormous shroud of fear and began to shake. I didn't know what to do. My parents were at work and my older brothers no longer lived at home. I looked to the windows and doors to see if they were open or closed. Did this guy know where I lived? Was he watching me right now? My parents wouldn't be home for hours. Did he know that my parents worked all the time? I just wanted off the call, but instead of slamming down the phone, I stood there almost frozen, barely breathing.

"No, thanks," I said flatly. "I don't want to do that."

There was a short silence at the other end. He was still talking but I couldn't really hear him because my heartbeat was slamming in my head so loudly, it almost drowned out the sound of his voice.

"I see . . . . Well, listen, no need to mention this call to your mom and dad . . ."

Of course, he didn't want my dad, or anyone in the neighborhood to know that he was hitting on a young teenage girl to exploit in his magazine! I made some quick excuse and hung up the phone. I didn't feel safe. *What can I do to protect myself?* I remember locking all the doors and checking the locks on the windows. A wave of questions soon followed. How did he know my name? How did this guy get our number? Would he call again, or worse, come over here? I didn't know if the man could see me in my house, or if he was one of the neighbors in our new neighborhood. Suddenly, I was suspicious of every man I didn't know.

It bothered me a lot that someone in my neighborhood was publishing that kind of magazine. I didn't even want to go outside because I didn't know who he was, where he was, or what he looked like. Had he called other girls in the neighborhood? Did he know that I was only thirteen? It was only much later in my life that I found out that Larry Flynt was the infamous publisher of the pornographic *Hustler* magazine. I learned later that many parents thought he lived too near Columbus School for Girls for their comfort, and they expressed concerns for their daughters' safety.

It was weird how seeing that name brought it all back. Had I known at that age what I knew while standing in Cochrane's that day, I would have reacted very differently. Interestingly, that wouldn't be my only reminder of predatory overtures. While still working at Cochrane's, one of my oldest brother's "friends" came walking into the store, triggering yet another memory. He had come to a party at our house while my mom was away. I was still very young at the time and had trusted him because he was Tom's friend. We were just talking, but then I realized he had me cornered. He attempted a sexual move on me. I wasn't interested, and I managed to get away from him. I was barely a teenager at the time. Again, I had been really afraid. When he came sauntering into Cochrane's, I was no longer that scared little girl, and I called him out. "Oh my God! This guy . . ." I said aloud with a dismissive gesture. All these people were standing in the aisles watching.

He remembered me and came walking up to me. "Hi Helen, how are you?"

"Don't even talk to me." I turned to my work, keeping him in view.

"What?" he asked throwing his hands wide in fake innocence. (Did I mention my brother had been in a gang?)

I stopped working and looked right at him. I did not speak quietly to protect his feelings. I had done nothing wrong then, and I was doing nothing wrong now. "You know exactly why! You know what you did and what you tried to do to me."

Not wanting to be spotlighted any more than he already was, he didn't stick around. It was empowering to me to call him out publicly and stand up for myself. Through that incident I found a measure of closure for both experiences. Had the magazine publisher shown up, I was confident I would have done the same thing to him. Clearly, I had taken the right path in getting involved with martial arts.

Those were confidence-building times for me, and it became easier to voice my opinions and defend my point of view. It didn't have to be like everyone else's. I no longer had to go along with the crowd, or popular thinking. I was allowed to think and act differently because I was a separate person. I had my own likes and dislikes, although some of them I guarded very carefully, depending on who was around me at the time. If I couldn't gauge the people around me, I kept my opinions to myself.

I was still uncomfortable with the idea of revealing my true self to my mom. She never pried. To date, the only person that ever expressed curiosity about me and Kristy was Kristy's aunt in Florida. She was actually the only person to ask Kristy a pointed but gently phrased question. "Are you and Helen more than friends?"

I don't know that Kristy ever directly answered, but Mom never asked. I began thinking it was necessary to come out to Mom, and Kristy and I talked about it for a long time. We agreed that I would tell her. One day, I was sitting on the bed between Mom and Kristy, all of us having a conversation. Just as the words were gathering on the tip of my tongue, Kristy nudged me, indicating that she had changed her mind, and I dropped it.

But my mom was very intuitive. Despite being discreet and undemonstrative, somehow, she still knew. In all the years that followed, Mom and I never discussed my preferences. I may have thought that I was doing a great job of keeping it hidden. But later, my niece told me a story about my nephew. In the company of my mom, he told a gay joke and Mom disapproved. I took it as her way of defending me. She may even have lost some friends over it. I was at an age where if her friends passed out of her life, I wasn't aware of it. If she did know I was gay, it was never mentioned to me. I'm sure my mom knew a great many things I never heard about.

As soon as we were able, Kristy and I got an apartment together. Despite my growing discontent, I focused my attention on getting my life into a rhythm and considered career possibilities. I settled into the same routine that had worked for me before: leaving campus and going directly to work or martial arts classes. Finishing college turned out to be a nonevent. I didn't go to the ceremony and there was no graduation party. I never connected with anyone in my classes. I was older than most of my classmates and only there to finish, not socialize. The university sent my diploma through the mail. I ticked the box for having kept my promise and went right on with my life.

I found a better-paid job as a receiving clerk at a building materials place, a job I had done in Florida. I knew I could turn that department around and have it running efficiently and effectively if I could just be given the opportunity. All I had to do was pass a forklift operator test to get my license. And I did. The store manager made me receiving supervisor.

Receiving was another job that empowered me because I learned a new skill and took over what had formerly been a man's job. I worked with another woman, the first time they'd ever had women in that department. I was organized, removed pallets from semi trailers, and between me and my assistant, we were able to maintain the inventory, price merchandise, and get it out on the floor more quickly than our predecessors. It was one of the best jobs I had had, and like Cochrane's, it was because of the people I was fortunate to work with.

With a different goal in mind, I returned to martial arts. Now the reason was no longer about defending myself. I wanted to compete at national and international levels and train for the upcoming 1988 Olympics. Upon my return to Columbus, I made the decision to train at a different martial arts school. Part of the reason I chose not to return to Master Choi's was I felt embarrassed about being gone so long and I didn't want to answer the many questions I'm sure my friends would have. In this other school I felt I could focus on my training without all of the emotional distractions. I wanted to be an Olympian.

To be considered for Olympic tryouts, the instructor must be affiliated with a specific organization. Unfortunately, this particular school I chose didn't have the credentials I needed to qualify for the US team. I left immediately and realigned with Master Choi, who was a highly respected Taekwondo master and closely affiliated with the Olympics. He was even elected to be the women's US Olympic team coach! He was the best of the best and he was my master teacher.

I also reconnected with my amazing friend Sunny, who had started a women's martial arts class called Feminists and Self-defense Training (FIST) at the Ohio State University's campus. She invited me to meet her students and check out the wonderful school. It was inspiring. The group consisted of OSU students, professors, and young career women, the majority of whom were lesbians. I found them extremely intimidating because this was the first time I had been exposed to women who were so comfortable with their sexuality. This was exactly what I needed to see.

"I'm not a feminist," I said to Sunny.

"What?! Yes, you are!"

Clearly, I was on a new learning curve. I had changed one dramatic thing in my life, and I had yet to see and understand how it affected every aspect of my life. It wasn't that everything I knew before had to be thrown out, but all my beliefs and ideas would need to pass through this new filter one by one and be scrutinized anew.

Not only was Sunny a great fighter, she was also a public defender. Eventually she gave up being a public defender because it was totally against the grain of who she was. As a bra-burning activist and war protester in the 70s, she went on to become one of the founders of Women Against Rape and Fan the Flames Bookstore, which was a feminist book boutique. Sunny was instrumental in helping me break out of my shell to discover and embrace who I actually am. She was a great mentor to me, and I wanted to be her friend. She didn't let people get close to her for many years, but, somehow, she let me in. We are still very close to this day.

I met a young woman there who was part of that organization, whom I will call Joanne. She and I shared a lot of similarities: we were both very outgoing, physically active, and interested in the same sports. We became fast friends and started hanging out and just having fun. She invited me to meet her at her house, then head over to a court to play racquetball at the Park of Roses. When I knocked on the door, Joanne's girlfriend answered, surprising me. I didn't think about what us hanging out together looked like to her because Joanne and I were just friends. Her girlfriend, Michelle, said very little. It was the first time I had met her, and she hardly talked. Something about the whole interaction was uncomfortable, but I didn't know what to do about it. Joanne came to the door, and we left. I didn't find out until much later why Michelle had been quiet.

"You know, I met you before," Michelle said.

"Really?"

Then she told me the whole story of how we'd met at an annual event called the National Women's Martial Arts Federation. Michelle had been practicing Taekwondo too. She said we were partnered up. I couldn't recall being her partner. She said she could hardly speak to me then because she was nervous and could not believe I was standing at her front door.

"Oh my gosh, I had no idea!" I said.

When she opened the front door and saw me standing there, she got tongue-tied all over again. Her inability to talk to me had nothing to do with my going out with her girlfriend, Joanne. Michelle had really strong feelings for me and said when she saw me, her heart skipped a beat. But she struggled to keep her feelings from showing.

At the time, my current relationship with Kristy was unresolved. Until I navigated my way out of it, I wasn't looking for another relationship. I had not pursued anyone, choosing to let things occur on their own. My thinking was that the people who were supposed to be in my life would somehow make themselves known to me. Sometimes that had unexpected results.

Since I was still new to the whole lesbian scene, I didn't know I was being hit on until someone else said so. "Oh yeah, she was hitting on you!" Or it had to be smack-dab in my face, like someone kissing me on the lips. Then I'd be like, "Whoa! What happened?" It always came as a surprise. I wondered how long it would take to get the hang of this new landscape. Lesbian relationships are complicated, and I had the hardest time figuring them out. There was so much to learn.

Meanwhile, I thought of every possible way to amicably break up with Kristy and keep her as a friend. Five years gave me a lot of time to think about the direction of where I wanted my life to go. I told her my truth of needing to move on. Although it was very sad, we separated and she moved back to Florida. We stayed in contact for a few years, then, as life would have it, we fell out of touch.

When Michelle and Joanne broke up, that was a difficult time for all three of us. Each of us lost someone in that deal, and that was hard to accept. But along the way, I became very interested in massage therapy. And someone new became interested in me.

Chapter 11

Full Contact

"The martial arts inspire power. Not power over, but power to:
To change, to fight back, to believe in oneself."
~ Anonymous

Michelle and I began spending more time together and discovered that we had a lot in common. Both of us had been raised by mothers who immigrated to America, Michelle's mother having been born in Scotland. We shared many other similarities in our nontraditional American families, and that understanding meant a lot to both of us. Michelle was fascinating and her intelligence was only outshined by her quirky, disarming sense of humor. She was also into martial arts which was a huge plus, and she supported me as I competed at increasingly higher levels. That was new for me, and the best of all possible worlds were coming together. I was in love and this felt right. I had never had my own personal cheerleader in martial arts or any sports previously. But Michelle understood the commitment, the training, and what it would take to become Olympic gold material. It was really a very special time. With that degree of encouragement, I believed that I could do anything.

Having mastered forms and point fighting in martial arts, I no longer did them. That page had turned, and that chapter was now closed. With Michelle by my side, I was ready to write a new chapter: full-contact fighting. During training, I had gone to the Olympic Training Center for a sports massage. I couldn't believe how quickly my body responded and recovered. It turned out to be very beneficial, faster than soaking, saunas, or anything else I had tried up to that point. It seemed nothing short of miraculous. As a result, I became very interested in the science of massage therapy.

During the Olympic tryouts, one of my teammates got badly hurt; he thought he'd have to drop out. He could hardly stand on his foot. With the limited time he had before his next match, Master Choi took him and our teammates behind the bleachers. Master Choi pulled out a set of needles to perform acupuncture on the man's foot and ankle area. It worked so quickly and so well he went to his next match favoring his one good foot. The opponent came at him, and he landed a kick to the opponent's face, knocking him out and winning the match. He was selected to be on the US Olympic team, where he later won a bronze medal!

That was eye-opening. I remember thinking these alternative medicines were exactly what I wanted to learn and provide to others. I must have shared these experiences with Michelle because one day she mentioned having seen something about a massage class. I thought we could offer this on the side, as part of our martial arts events. Together we went to a public school facility and signed up for classes to get massage therapy training and licenses. At that time, massage therapy was a cottage industry and most massage therapists worked out of their homes, fitness studios, chiropractic offices or salons. Soon we developed our own unique idea: we wanted to create a clinic environment specific to body work. This would be our source of income, and we would be working together while helping people. It sounded like a win-win.

Meanwhile, Master Choi began training a handful of us to be elite fighters. I was very disciplined. If I had to train until I puked, I would do it. When I was a red belt, I started competing nationally.

Competing in full-contact fighting requires being a black belt. Master Choi gave me one because he knew that I was talented enough to fight. My natural weight put me at the flyweight division, which is from 94.5 to 105 lbs. In that division, my opponents would have been taller than me. He wanted me to move down to the finweight division which gave me the advantage. To get there, I had to lose close to ten pounds on my four-foot-eleven frame. I just did what my coach told me to do. If Master Choi wanted me to compete in a specific weight category, I had to make it happen.

How we lost weight was not very healthy. In the process, I lost my period. I got dizzy from starving. It took me a while, but I got used to it. Having to lose weight like that the first time, and then compete, was difficult, because I love food. Master Choi also didn't want our fight team members competing in the same weight divisions. Doug, Chris, Jennifer, and I had to lose weight. One guy named Greg had to go up a weight class, which meant he had to gain.

To compete in the United States, you can weigh in at the beginning of your tournament, then go replenish fluids or have a meal before your match. I could weigh in on a Friday, go eat, and fight on Saturday without being reweighed. At the international level, they don't allow that. You weigh in the same day you fight, which is really tough. My teammates and I trained three times a day, five days a week. We went to breakfast and dinner together. Most of us didn't eat. We used to go to Wendy's when they had a salad buffet. We'd get salad with nothing on it. Then Greg, who had to gain weight, would eat in front of us and gorge himself. He literally wanted to throw up after he ate because he was miserable, and the rest of us needed to throw up to lose weight. Before the day of the fight, we sat in plastic garbage bags in a sauna trying to sweat out all the excess water and spitting into our Dixie cups. Collectively, we were just crabby. At some points we got to where we didn't like each other, at least not until we could eat normally. None of us wanted to disappoint the team.

I also trained solo to perfect my techniques. I didn't have natural God-given talent, but I was very dedicated to being a good fighter in training. Once I commit to doing something, I will see it through to the end. I believed that I could accomplish anything if I focused my energy in the right way. However, one bad habit took root that would dog me for many years afterward. When I saw food, I'd be struck with a ferocious appetite. Often, I'd over-indulge until my stomach hurt, and I was so uncomfortable that I had to sleep sitting up. I didn't talk about it with anyone. I was ashamed that I struggled with self-control in that area. I didn't know what to do about it. Until I figured it out, I kept it to myself and focused on staying as active as I could to burn off the calories.

By focusing on full-contact fighting, I competed at higher and higher levels—the regional tournaments and national competitions. I then set my sights on the most coveted achievement of all: the US Olympic Taekwondo team. To compete on that level, all candidates are required to go through regional tryouts, then fight at the national level and win one of the top three placements. I won in the regionals and went straight to the nationals.

Back when I competed in the 1981 Nationals, just before going to Florida, I had been matched with the two-time National Champion in my weight division. Her name was Cheryl. We competed against each other in full-contact fighting—my first match there, her third. She got the gold, and I won the silver. In the years before my return, Cheryl remained on the US Taekwondo Team, winning a total of ten national awards, but never placing internationally. When I came back on the scene in 1987, Cheryl was still competing. When we faced each other again, I saw that she recognized me. She was now the undefeated ten-time US National Champion in my weight division. In 1987, I beat her and won the national title and the gold medal, and she was out. Then I defeated her in the 1988 Nationals as well. But because life is full of surprises, the next time would be life changing for both of us. The Olympic tryouts came later that year and a chance to be on the 1988 US Olympic Team. According to the rules of the US Taekwondo Team and the Olympic Committee, my opponent and I had both met all the requirements and qualified to compete.

I wanted that more than anything, and, by the way she fought, she did too. We fought every one of our opponents with a vengeance, so that we could compete against each other at the Olympic finals. She was just as determined to beat me as I was to defeat her. By the time we had ousted everyone else, Master Choi explained that she was the incumbent, and the committee was going to choose her unless I made the win obvious. *Obvious?*

"In order for you to get on the team," he said, "you need to knock her out." She and I wanted to go to the Olympic Games more than anything. This was the determining match, and I had to make it count. I stubbornly gave it everything I had. Every ounce of me went into every jump kick, every reverse punch, and every counter move. I wanted to keep moving until one of us wasn't, and that needed to be her. Then suddenly everything stopped. The match was so close that some people thought I had won. In fact, the match was so close that Master Choi ponied up the money to contest it and have it arbitrated. I wasn't able to knock her out. The committee didn't budge from their (pre-determined) decision. My opponent had won.

Disappointment burned my throat. I wanted my face to be inscrutable as I gave her the good, sportsman-like bow. Inside, the defeat felt like iron straps around my chest, and I could hardly breathe. Nothing is as bitter as being robbed of victory. I knew that I should have won. I knew I was good enough, as did Master Choi. What made the loss so devastating and hard to accept was knowing that, if there had been no bias, I would have the title "Best in the USA."

Though it was of little consolation at the time, I was made an Olympic alternate. The ache of defeat proved difficult to shake off. People rallied around me. They insisted I shouldn't be disappointed because I was still part of the Olympic team. If she got injured, or any mishap should befall her, I would be going to the Olympics. One friend even offered to cause a "mishap" not unlike the event that occurred several years later, where a figure skater destroyed her Olympic chances when she conspired to attack a talented fellow skater two days before Olympic trials. I appreciated my friend's loyalty, but declined. I wanted my win acknowledged through proper channels.

It took a long time for me to be proud of becoming an alternate. An "A" team and "B" team were formed. The A team went to the 1988 Summer Olympics in Seoul, Korea. The B team, the alternates, would normally have gone to the Olympics as well. But that year, Taekwondo was a demonstration sport which was performed specifically to promote its acceptance during the Olympic Games. They decided against taking alternates, another bitter disappointment.

In 1989, I was invited to the Olympic Sports Festival taking place in Oklahoma City. Before heading out to that competition, I came down with strep throat. I went to my doctor, who strongly advised me not to go, but a lot was riding on this event: sponsorships, medals, acclaim, and the chances it affords. I also needed to assuage my bruised ego.

"Oh no, I'm going." I was so dedicated to going that only death itself would prevent me from attending.

"Strep throat can affect your heart," she sharply cautioned.

It wasn't that I didn't believe her, it was that I knew I only had so many opportunities left to compete, and I didn't want to miss any of them. At twenty-nine, some already considered me past my prime. "I'll take my chances."

"Well, let's at least prescribe some medications."

"I can't take any medications because they do drug testing."

My doctor was not happy. I went anyway, sick and feeling awful. As a result, I didn't do very well, but I did win a bronze medal.

One benefit of reaching the level of Olympic alternate was revealed the following year in 1990, when I was invited to compete in the fourth World Cup Taekwondo—the first Women's World Cup Taekwondo—in Madrid, Spain. We were required to go there a few weeks before the competition to get acclimated and train together as a team. These games were just as competitive as the Olympics. The sponsors had sent me to be on the team with all the fighters that competed in Seoul in 1988. I was able to compete with the winners who would have been in my weight division.

The gold and silver medalists were there, and about thirty or forty countries were represented.

The hard thing was having to lose weight and watch every bite I ate. I knew I could lose a pound, or maybe a pound and a half, before the day of my weigh-in and the match. International committees are very strict, and, with no small effort, I really paid attention to every mouthful. A young seventeen- or eighteen-year-old woman in the flyweight division was traveling for the first time out of the country. She fell in love with the bread. "You better slow down!" I warned. "You still have to weigh in." She must have thought she was training hard enough to burn it all off. But, on the day of her first fight, she'd gained a pound or more and was promptly disqualified. She was shocked and very disappointed, as was the United States Taekwondo Union (USTU, formerly AAU) who was footing the bill for us to be there.

The training schedule was grueling: getting up at 5am to go running as a team, then go work out and run practice drills three times a day. There was really nothing but that to do. However, our team did manage to squeeze in some sightseeing before the games began. While we were there, we wore our team jackets with USA embroidered on them. On that trip, I noticed that people from other parts of the world were not thrilled about Americans. When certain people saw us, they spat on the ground. "Bah! Americans!"

Despite this animosity, we proudly participated in the opening ceremony, where each group marched in a procession with their top athletes carrying their country's flag. During the day and into the evening, I watched and participated in many fights. It was exciting to be among such talented athletes. In one fight, I was matched against the Olympic bronze medalist from Korea. I had to fight her because the gold medalist from Chinese Taipei had beat her. I fought the bronze medalist and won, which landed me in the finals. Then, after fighting one match after another all day, came the final match for the gold in the finweight division. Our last match was between me and the gold medalist from Chinese Taipei.

People from other countries can train full time. A lot of American athletes can't. Trying to get sponsors, work, and train was really challenging. It became clear that my opponent had been training full time. And, oh my God, I never fought anyone who was so lickety-split fast! I mean, she came in with a jump-axe kick. I blocked it. She came down while I scrambled around the ring trying to get my bearings. She was just amazing. Chinese Taipei won the gold. I was proud to win the silver medal.

At the award ceremony immediately following, I stood on the podium with the winners to be awarded a medal. I barely noticed my hand throbbing. It wasn't until after the ceremony that I really looked at it. My hand and my finger were twisted at an unnatural angle. I thought, *That's weird*. When I moved it, it hurt! Something wasn't right because it kept twisting back to this strange position. I waited until after the ceremony and then found the US team doctor and showed it to him. "What's going on with my hand?"

"Oh! We need to take you to the medical table."

Well, the medical guy didn't speak English. He tried to communicate with me in Spanish while he sprayed cold aerosol liniment on my hand. That made it feel much better almost immediately. He massaged my hand muscles for a few moments. Then, all of a sudden, the coldness wore off.

"AHHH! That doesn't feel right!" I grimaced. The team doctor returned. "This does not feel right." I showed him my hand.

"Oh my God! Don't massage that," he advised. "It's probably broken."

My last match had been so quick, I hadn't realized that my opponent had caused a spiral fracture in a metacarpal bone in my hand. The team doctor took me to the hospital in Madrid. They led us downstairs into a basement area, which they called the hospital. It looked like Dr. Frankenstein's lab: eerie and scary and dank. But they wrapped my hand and put a cast on it, which was great, but it felt tight.

That night I could tell something was amiss. I got ahold of our team doctor once more and told him something was wrong with my hand. He again looked it over. "Oh wow. Let's get you back over there."

At the hospital, he told them the cast was on too tight and that my blood was not circulating to my fingers. They pulled out this thing that looked like a small circular saw with no blade guard. Placing my cast hand on an examination table, they started cutting into the cast.

"That hurts," I said. I kept trying to move away.

"Don't move," the doctor said.

"Yeah, but I think you're cutting into my hand."

When they finally got the cast off, there was a red mark on my hand where they were cutting through the cast to my skin. I was no longer confident that they could help me and just wanted to get out of there. The team doctor had also seen enough.

"Let us recast it," the Madrid doctor said.

"No, no, no, no, no. Just give me some splints," the team doctor insisted. "We'll take care of her when we get back to the States."

After a whole month away, I had become homesick. The States sounded like some faraway promised land. I just wanted to go home and be surrounded by familiar people and familiar foods and have a burger! Comfort food! As I flew out of Spain with the team, I was happy to have won a silver medal and happy to have been able to compete with the top athletes in the world, but I was not feeling quite as great as when I had arrived there. My hand throbbed in the high altitude. When the specialist in Columbus saw my hand, he wanted to operate immediately and install plates and pins.

"No, please try to fix it without any kind of surgery. My livelihood is massage therapy, and I can't have all of that going on."

He created an appliance to keep my hand stabilized and protected, which prevented my ring finger from twisting. Unlike a cast, I could remove it if I had to. Even though I had to wear it longer, I was thrilled to avoid surgery. Sometimes even now, when I push open a door, I occasionally experience sharp pains, but I did eventually regain full use of my hand. A new little voice had appeared, though, and I didn't like the message. *You're getting too old for this*. I quickly relegated it to negative thinking and ignored it. I kept on training every day, a thousand kicks a day. I wasn't ready to give up competing yet. You may have heard that the little voice doesn't like being ignored. For a time, it may even grow louder. Wisdom says the little voice eventually wins. The question was, how long and at what cost would I ignore it?

Chapter 12

Yin & Yang

"Health and well being can be achieved only by remaining centered in spirit, guarding against the squandering of energy, promoting the constant flow of Qi and blood, maintaining harmonious balance of yin and yang, adapting to the changing seasonal and yearly macrocosmic influences and nourishing oneself preventatively. This is the way to a long and happy life."
~ The Yellow Emperor's Classic of Internal Medicine

In the nature of things there is a duality of energies which complement each other. The two opposing forces are Yin and Yang. The Yin-Yang symbol represents the philosophy of Taoism. Examples of these opposing energies are male and female energies, sun and moon, push and yield, and many more which are replicated in our external as well as our internal environment. The Yin-Yang does not necessarily represent good and evil energies. When this cosmic duality of energies is in balance they exist in perfect harmony. If there is an imbalance, then disease, illness, and injuries can occur within the body.

I experienced the depletion of the Yin energy in my body during the stressful preparation for competition, which included the need to starve myself to qualify to compete in my weight division, my body developing a pattern of coming down with strep throat just prior to a match. Major stress and lack of nutrients can deplete the body of energy causing an imbalance. Because of the symptoms I knew I had to shift from "doing" to "being." In taking up Tai Chi and Qi Gong, it allowed for my Yin energy to be nourished in mind, body, and spirit. The more I understood the power of these energies, the more Michelle and I began to focus on opening our massage clinic in an effort to help others to restore the balance of Qi in their bodies.

Once Michelle and I became licensed massage therapists, we successfully opened our first clinic, Massage Away Inc. Around this same time, we began gathering information on various schools and clinics all over the country, and Michelle and I discovered a mutual love of traveling. She excelled in organizing trips for us, and we visited many states and several countries. We traveled around to see how other massage schools were set up. We could write it off as research!

We opened a second clinic a few years later. Our tagline was "Massage away the pain, the stress, the madness." Then we got in trouble with the Psychiatric Board. They said we couldn't use "the madness" because that was their turf. So, we dropped that tag line.

The first year in our professional clinic, we rented space in a pricey medical facility. It gave us instant credibility and separated us from the shady massage parlor image. Our model was to build up our contracted therapist's clientele and accept a certain percentage from their sales, which enabled the business to run and made it possible for me and Michelle to get away and take time off. Eventually, we found a better priced facility and began spreading the word.

As we worked with our therapists, Michelle and I realized there was a huge gap in their training. Beginning a business with only book knowledge made for a very nerve wracking experience for new therapists. When they landed their first client, it was their first time practicing what they learned on a live, paying body. It was frustrating to realize that most therapists also had little business knowledge. They didn't understand how to run a business, nor did they comprehend the ethics of maintaining business hours—you don't knock off work just because it's a beautiful day! We were constantly short staffed because they wanted to call off or duck out early. We would then have to pick up or reschedule missed appointments and explain to clients why their therapists weren't in. This caused problems for everyone. Michelle and I came up with several ideas that would fix these problems and approached the massage training school. We suggested implementing additional programs that would help new therapists effectively run their new enterprise, like business management, marketing, and, more importantly, a student clinic where students could take all the knowledge they were learning and apply it to live people while being supervised. We were surprised when the school declined our suggestion and showed no interest in holding the student clinics. They were only interested in teaching the basics and finer points of massage.

After that meeting ended, my entrepreneurial spirit kicked in. They hadn't so much rejected our idea as handed us the business opportunity of a lifetime, and I decided to take a chance. "We can do this," I said to Michelle. "We can start our own school and pass on the knowledge that we learned and what made us successful." So that's what we did. In the early 1990s no one in the country was doing clinics the way we were. It turns out our model was very easy to duplicate, and, in the years following, it would be increasingly popular.

Meanwhile, in 1991, I was invited to the US Olympic Festival, in Anaheim, California. The top four US athletes in the country in each category gathered at this national event to compete. All the Olympic sports were represented. As part of the opening ceremony, all the athletes parade in, smiling and waving, representing their sport. The sponsors—Mars, Incorporated being one of them—gave us a lot of nice gifts suited to our sport: Pine Tree uniforms, Adidas kicking shoes and paddles, US Olympic Festival Team warm-up suits, and a bunch of their candy.

Taekwondo is a lot like a chess game. You want to have a strategy and know what your opponent's moves are, three moves ahead.

The sport is very physical but psychological as well. Experience plus all I had learned in martial arts taught me to strategize, not react. It's imperative to have presence of mind, and the ability to harness the mental strength to execute the strategy. That's why, years later, when I saw the gunman in my car, I knew to quickly create a strategy. Panicking prevents the mind from thinking rationally. Because there isn't much time to think in a ring, you must be able to get calm and assess your opponent instantly. It's similar to thinking on our feet when unexpected life situations pop up. If I control my emotions, I can ask myself, *What can I do here? What's my plan?* I can quickly come to sound conclusions. That's true whether I'm in the ring, in a street fight, or in a car hold up.

Master Choi's elite fighter training was so intense that a couple of times I skipped a promotion by learning the equivalent of two belts simultaneously, then double testing. Despite all my black belt training, every time I stepped into the ring for a full-contact tournament, I was scared because we were trying to knock each other out or knock out each other's teeth. The butterflies in my stomach always came, but part of my fighting strategy was knowing how to control them and channel that energy to my advantage.

After brutal schedules, working hard, and practicing fight drills while maintaining sharp focus, we were given the most wonderful break, a team-building outing to Disneyland! That was such a festive occasion, and immensely refreshing to have a playday to just be and have fun with my team. It remains one of my fondest memories of our time there.

At the Anaheim tournament, I won the bronze medal, but I couldn't help notice something was off in my body. I didn't believe that I was too old to compete. I still felt healthy and fit. I did notice that the losing and gaining weight cycle affected my relationship with food. I could stuff myself at all-you-can-eat buffets or eat a whole pizza or cake by myself. Then, not only would I feel awful physically and mentally, I'd beat myself up for eating so much. During these binges I thought there was something wrong with me. I couldn't understand how I could be so disciplined with so many things—such as my training, my schedule, and my other commitments—but had such little control over my eating. Why couldn't I stop when I no longer felt hungry? It was only when women began talking about anorexia and bulimia that I realized I had developed an eating disorder. I eventually stopped losing weight to compete.

Then, my very close friend Sunny confided in me that she had an eating disorder. It's a very serious condition that is extremely hard on the body and can sometimes result in death. I believe that she went on to get the proper treatment and eventually gained control of her eating habits. I was able to be more intentional about portion control and what I ate. A tactic that has served me well is to avoid getting too hungry, especially if there are plans to order out. If I wait until I'm too hungry, I tend to order too much and then find myself eating leftovers the rest of the week. I didn't recognize at the time how these extremes in eating affected my overall health and vitality.

In 1992, I pressed my luck for another chance at the gold, despite being thirty-two and what many consider too old to compete. I participated successfully in regionals and went to the national competitions again. Since it was an Olympic year, record numbers of people came out of the woodwork to compete, dreaming of Olympic fame. Even though I had been racked with strep throat at every competition, now I was also plagued by injuries. As an older athlete, I began to recognize that I needed to stop before I pushed it too far. Before long, I would be forced to admit my body was saying, "That's it."

In a competition, I was matched with Shawna, who was young and fast. Because I hadn't lost weight to compete, the very thing Master Choi had hoped to avoid now stared me in the face—she was tall. I didn't let myself be psyched out by that. I made my usual quick assessments and strategies. In a jump-spin-wheel kick, she caught me on the left temple. I went down seeing stars. I shot back up, dismissing the referee's concerns. I said I was just fine, but the ref was unconvinced. Even though I finished that match and left under the power of my own feet, getting carried out on a stretcher was something I wanted to avoid at all costs. Strep throat followed me to every competition, and I either didn't understand or refused to see what was happening inside my body.

For all my effort, I was awarded a certificate of participation for the Olympic trials. Taekwondo had taken me to where I felt satisfied with competing on an international level. The opportunities that had come my way as a result of being an Olympic alternate had been amazing after all. I felt like I had reached the end of a chapter and I didn't want to compete anymore.

I didn't burn any bridges with Master Choi, which, for him, was very unusual. He'd grow many fighters to an elite level, and then there would be a falling out. It's important for me to treat others the way I want to be treated. While growing up, people weren't very kind to me, and I know how that feels and how important it is to be kind. I believe that all relationships are valuable. They don't always have to serve us. Everyone has their own stuff going on. Even if we go our separate ways, we can still be kind to one another. I may not agree with everyone, but I can still respect them and value them. Eventually, I told Master Choi how much I had always wanted to learn Kung Fu because of its Chinese heritage. He seemed to understand and gave me his blessing. I was proud of the fact that he left that door open for me.

I practiced a Wah Lum Kung Fu system for about four years. I still perform the annual Lion Dance with them during Chinese New Year. I also trained in several other disciplines including Bando, the Burmese martial arts system, up to second-degree black belt.

I had gained a lot of knowledge, and conferences, camps, and workshops continued to give me opportunities to teach and maintain ties to the martial arts family. It was at a martial arts conference where I met Master Wen Mei Yu, one of the Qigong Masters who taught in a particular style. She noticed me and said that my Chi was depleted in the Yin aspect but very strong in the Yang, causing an imbalance within my bio-magnetic field. I had no idea what she was talking about or what it meant. We became friends, and she encouraged me to learn her style of Qigong and practice Tai Chi. Though I would practice several additional disciplines, these would be my go-to exercises for many years. It was another full circle moment, as I remembered my grandfather's invitations to join him in Tai Chi. Maybe what he'd seen was a hyper kid learning to trust that energy. In his own way, he may have been informing me that my energy would only carry me so far. During my Taekwondo days, I had no idea that I was on a trajectory of slowly and consistently depleting my Yin. I began noticing a dramatic improvement after listening to Master Yu.

Tai Chi and Qigong, which are internal martial arts disciplines, strengthened my Chi field, the inner reserves and vitality which are in all living things. Some people have more than others. Now when I teach, I share this wisdom and knowledge. "Do not squander your energy," I tell my students. "Whether it's physical, mental, or emotional. Stress drains energy to a point where illness and disease can occur." It's likely that my grandfather knew this all along. Although he passed away in 1984, I like to think that somewhere in the spirit realm he is smiling and pleased that I finally figured out what he wanted to show me.

One other extremely important thing I learned from him before he left this earth was to appreciate people and relationships. Up until I fought competitively, the families of other martial artists came along to cheer us on. Victories are so much sweeter and more meaningful when shared with people who understand the sport, who care about you, and who encourage you through the process. They see how far you've come. They know all the effort and sweat that went into learning new moves and moving up a level. They're happy right along with you. And you can be happy with them in their victories also, because you appreciate all that goes into their win. Though, over time, people left, moved, or just went their separate ways, even now, some of my closest friends are from that martial arts family. We had this great camaraderie.

However, with tournaments off the table, it was time for me to explore how to grow our business. I had dreams for a different type of school, and I began focusing my energy on loftier goals.

Helen Yee flies through workout in tae kwon do, hoping for spot on U.S. Olympic team

This 95-pounder deals real kick

By Lee Stratton
Helen Yee weighs 95 pounds and has a

another martial arts instructor; and Jennifer Gray, 16, a junior at Westerville North High School.

"It builds up confidence and teaches respect, modesty and humbleness.

Article in local paper before the Olympic trials

I win gold medal at the 1988 Nationals

Helen Yee of Columbus re-
ceives gold medal in fin-
weight division. She defeated Cheryl Kalanoc to win
her second straight national
title.

Newspaper article following my second
straight National title

Taekwondo Times 1988 Olympic Issue

ONE MASTER'S HARVEST OF CHAMPIONS

By Michael McFarlane

Five students from one school all qualified for the Olympic Team Trials at Colorado Springs last June. What special formula does Master Choi of Columbus, Ohio, have that yields this crop champions?

What does it take to become a national Tae Kwon Do champion? Maybe a quick roundhouse, a couple of head fakes and a balanced spinning wheel kick? How about a triple-somersaulting, double-twisting, front kick with a real loud kiap?

If it isn't fancy techniques, maybe it's superior athletic ability. Maybe the champions all have some mystical muscle fibers that allow them to deliver their kicks and punches faster than the speed of light.

Students at the Oriental Martial Arts College (OMAC) in Columbus, Ohio, seem to have discovered the secret of winning in competitive Tae Kwon Do. Five students from OMAC qualified for the Olympic team tryouts this year in Miami, Florida. Three of the five students, Chris Spence, Doug Baker and Helen Yee, earned gold medals at the USTU National Championship last April. Competing as an adult, Jennifer Gray, 16, took a bronze and Greg Baker (Doug's older brother) was invited to the tryouts because of his outstanding record in other national and international competitions.

**Taekwondo Times 1988 Summer Issue
Oriental Martial Arts College's Proud
National Champions & Olympians**

Harvest of Champions

*Flying sidekick at Martial Arts
Training Camp*

*Teaching a complex pose at
a women's conference*

Teaching a martial arts form at a women's martial arts conference

Having fun teaching Dhanda Yoga

Chapter 13

That Inner Voice Again

One perk of being a long-term member of the martial arts community is being invited to teach at camps and conferences not only all over the United States, but in other countries like Germany and Greece. After teaching classes or workshops, I usually stick around and enjoy visiting the people, hanging out with the martial artists, and exploring the area. One time, after a martial arts camp, my friend Sunny, who had moved to Germany, met me on the Greek island of Paros. While we walked around, she noticed this moped place and wanted to rent one. "Come on, it will be fun! You can ride on the back," she said.

Though it sounded like a lot of fun, and the idea of letting someone else do all the work was appealing, I felt uneasy about sharing a bike. "I'd really rather have my own moped!"

"It will be more fun this way!" she pleaded. What I really believed was that the little voice was telling me to get my own bike. But she begged me. And pleaded some more. "Aw, come on! Please, please!" So, I gave into her.

Picture me riding on the back of a moped with my best friend. We zoomed past hot pink flowers spilling out of window boxes in beautiful, white-washed Greece in the tiny, tourist-congested streets. We were smiling and having a great time. While I took in the sights, I may have even been chastising myself for nearly missing out on this simple joy. But then, just as we were going into a turn, a tour bus clipped us.

I managed to quickly jump off the bike. Sunny fell and hit her head. As she lay in the middle of the street, I ran to her, but she wasn't moving. Grabbing one part of the moped and the muffler, I threw it off her. Blood was coming from under her helmet. *Oh my God! She's dead!*

Then I realized I was in a foreign country and didn't know the language, and we were in serious need of help. I could barely think of what to do. The tour bus had stopped, and people swarmed from it into the street. Someone called an ambulance. I feared an oncoming car would hit us. Somebody stopped traffic to prevent us from getting run over. Because we needed to get out of the street, I kept speaking to her. "Sunny, get up, get up!" But she didn't respond. *This can't be happening!* There in the middle of the street I heard voices all around me, but I didn't understand any of them. I believed that they were all trying to help in their own way, but I never felt so alone. *She can't be dead. She can't be.* "Sunny! Sunny!" Suddenly, her eyes opened, and her hand went to her head. She started to get up. *She's alive! Thank God she's alive!* I could breathe again.

"Wait, wait, hold still!" I said. I didn't want her to move until we knew how badly she was hurt. The ambulance arrived. The squad swept in with a gurney and spoke to her.

They clipped her in tight then hurried her into the belly of the ambulance, checking her vitals and looking at her injuries. After I got inside, they rushed to the hospital, sirens howling. She and I were both shaking. I kept talking to her to make sure she was staying with us. The whole left side of her body was skinned and scraped raw after sliding across the pavement. That was going to hurt, but I was incredibly grateful that she was alive. At the hospital, they ran a bunch of tests and thoroughly examined her for broken bones. They wanted to make sure she had no internal bleeding. After they got her taken care of, a doctor and nurse came to check me out, but I thought back to that dismal incident in Spain.

"No, thank you. I'm okay," I said.

"No, no," they insisted. "We need to check you over to know if you're okay."

"No, I'm really okay."

The doctor started getting mad at me. "It's required that I work on you. Otherwise, you must leave."

"Okay, I'll leave."

"Okay," he said. "But you might want to look at your arm."

Then I saw a big gashing hole in my elbow that was pouring blood. My hand was blistering. Now I understood why they wanted to give me stitches and a tetanus shot. I hadn't even noticed because my adrenaline was so pumped up, and I was in shock. But I really didn't want them looking me over. "Well, can I at least have a towel?" I asked.

They gave me a white towel, and I put my elbow in it. Then I went outside. I just sat in the parking lot trying to get myself together. As I considered all that had just happened, it hit me very hard how close I had come to losing a really dear friend. When I thought she was dead, I had been scared out of my mind. It could have been both of us. That really shook me. I had to calm myself down.

I looked at the situation in positives. I was deeply grateful that she was alive and despite major scrapes and bleeding, she was still intact. I was thankful I hadn't died or been seriously injured. Helpful people had instantly appeared. The staff had insisted on keeping Sunny overnight to monitor her condition. They were concerned about a possible concussion and internal bleeding. I wanted to believe she was going to be all right, which brought me back to the present moment. I was still sitting in the parking lot of a hospital somewhere in Greece. *Okay . . . what the hell am I going to do right now?* I was still trying to feel relieved. I wasn't even exactly sure where the hospital was in relation to our hotel, or the martial arts camp location, or how to get back.

The next thing I heard was someone speaking to me in English! It was as reassuring as a warm blanket when you're shivering with cold. Here I was in Greece, and I heard an American voice. I saw a young blonde walking toward me dressed in medical scrubs. It turns out she was a college student doing some kind of internship at the hospital. I felt like I was waking up out of a nightmare into safe, familiar surroundings.

"Wow, do you need any help?" she asked.

"Actually, I do."

As my shock slowly faded, the pain of my own injuries were making themselves felt and I knew I couldn't keep walking around with a towel on my elbow. The woman told me her name and that she was from Colorado. Next, she drove me to a pharmacy and bought me medical tape, gauze, bandages, aspirin, and some water. Then she drove me back to the location where the rest of my group was staying. That helped calm me down a lot. In a true moment of need, the right person had just materialized. At the hotel, I shared our mishap with the group. The next day, Sunny was released. From then on, I put a lot more trust in that inner voice. I was learning to pay attention, and very soon heeding that little voice would impact the trajectory of my business and personal life.

Chapter 14

Ghost Wedding

In 1994, piggybacking on name recognition, Massage Away School of Therapy was born. Our very first class had fourteen students!

As the school began to grow, Michelle and I closed one of our two clinics to focus on building our programs. Because students weren't allowed to get paid, we offered lower-priced massages to the public, which went directly to the school. Students then worked on those clients, which provided valuable experience and credit hours which are required for graduation. One other avenue was for students to take part at local events like the Special Olympics and the annual Columbus Marathon, which the school volunteered for. We set up our tables inside a medical tent, and students worked on people who had finished the race. These events drew elite, world-class runners locally and from as far away as Kenya. We were getting "free" advertising for our school, and people were able to see the kind of work we did and ask questions.

I highly admired and had great respect for these marathon runners. Although long-distance endurance running is not my sport, as an athlete, I've always kept some kind of exercise regimen: yoga, soccer, snowboarding, biking, or hiking. I know that movement is a key element for good health and wellbeing, even if just to move the energy in the body. I've always been healthy, and I like to move my body by either being in competitive or individual sports. Because I was in decent shape, one year I decided to challenge myself and see if I could run in the Columbus Marathon.

From my personal experience, I concluded that a marathon can be divided into two races. One part is the first twenty-six miles, and the second part, which was the most grueling for me, is the last fifth of a mile. It takes a long time to run that far. That's when you have to dig deep inside and find whatever you can to get through it to the finish line. That last point-two miles was excruciating. Even though I had done significant training for this race, my knee locked up. It was so challenging that when I saw the finish line, I literally cried. Oh my God, I was beyond happy to finish! My time was four hours and nineteen minutes. I'm glad I did it for the experience, but it nearly killed me. I have a huge level of appreciation for marathoners. I made a promise to myself and my body that I would never do that ever again! It's definitely not my sport.

Despite the positive upward growth of our school, not everything in my life was going well. I kept the promise that I made to myself to help Mom. Through Mom I learned that my older brothers worked at jobs, married, and had children. I didn't see them very often.

I hadn't seen Henry at all. On the surface, everything appeared to be fine. But when the word somehow traveled through our family that I was a lesbian, my oldest brother kept his daughter from spending time with me. Shelly and I had always been close. His decision hurt both of us. He didn't talk to me directly, but maybe my brother worried I would try to bend her thinking around to mine. He couldn't have been more wrong. I didn't have some personal agenda to convert every female to my lifestyle. Being in love with someone of my own sex didn't mean I was in love with all women and girls. Eventually he relented, and my niece and I were able to continue enjoying each other's company.

Whatever my youngest brother's opinions were of my life, he mostly kept to himself. Henry was still deeply troubled. Even after getting out of high school, he had not grown out of his partying ways and his addiction prevented him from moving forward and developing a rewarding life. Stealing from people to support his habit got him in trouble with family, the police, and his so-called friends. Without ambition, his life seemed to have stalled like a broken-down car in rush hour traffic. And Henry still lived at home.

None of this sat well with my mom. Mom was always worried about her youngest child, largely because he seemed so unlucky in life. Why could he never seem to catch a break? Each day she felt more weighed down until she unburdened her soul to a friend, sharing all the troubles of Henry's life. At the time, I knew nothing about this.

My mother's friend Elaine thought Mom might be anxious enough to consider measures outside of her Catholic faith. It was this very friend who talked my mother into seeing the fortune teller who was well known in the Chinese community. Mom was very skeptical but admittedly desperate. She finally agreed to go to Chicago with Elaine and pay this fortune teller a visit.

Despite her great reputation and high community respect, the fortune teller lived a very modest life. She worked in Chinatown as a humble dishwasher at a Chinese restaurant and refused payment for any of her readings. I can just imagine how it went . . . .

The three of them go to a quiet booth toward the back of the restaurant. My mother and her friend sit across from the fortune teller.

"I see you have a heavy heart and have traveled a great distance," the fortune teller says. "How can I help you?"

"It's my son."

"Let's have a cup of tea and you can concentrate on your question." A young girl brings a steaming pot and porcelain cups and sets them before the women. As the fortune teller pours the fragrant tea, she studies my mother's face. My mother concentrates very hard, trying not to give anything away. She guards her words carefully, not saying too much, because she wants to see if the fortune teller is legit. While staring at the tiny leaves floating in her cup, the fortune teller shakes her chi-chi sticks, and, when one jumps out, she reads it pensively. As the tea leaves slowly sink to the bottom of the thin white cup, the fortune teller shuffles a deck of cards and lays them out in a pattern on the table. When my mother's cup is nearly empty, the fortune teller takes it and swirls the dregs first one way, then another. Then she looks at my mother. "Your son is unlucky because the spirit of your dead son is jealous of him for living in this life, and he is haunting him."

My mom's eyes fly open in surprise. Her friend's mouth opens in shock. My mom has never told anyone about the son who died at birth the year before Henry was born! This convinces my mom that the fortune teller is authentic, and she asks further questions. "What can be done to stop the haunting? What can be done to help my son?"

When my mother got home, she told me and Michelle all that the fortuneteller had said. "You must find the dead spirit son a bride," the fortune teller had said. "Then he will be happy and stop haunting Henry."

After the long conversation with the fortune teller, my mother seemed more hopeful. Now that the problem had been figured out, she could form a plan. Ghost weddings are very popular—in fact, big business—in China, and she enlisted me and Michelle to help her find a spirit bride for her spirit son. She was so anxious for a change in Henry's luck that Michelle and I agreed at once to help her.

"What do you need?" I wanted to know.

"I'm glad you asked." She'd had a long ride back from Chicago to consider this. Between the fortune teller and her friend, Mom had the answer to get Henry's life back on track. "First, finding the right match that pleases the deity gods. That can only be decided through the Incense Burning Ceremony. Three incense sticks represent the deity gods. Once they are lit, if they burn down at the same time, then the spirit bride is a good match. However, if the incense does not burn down at the same time, then it is not."

"Mom, we can do the incense ceremony for Uncle Bo's daughter," I said, having a flash of recollection. "Didn't she die about the same year?"

"No. Not Uncle Bo's daughter," she said adamantly, shaking her head. "I don't want to be related to them!"

Michelle, Shelly, and I considered other friends of Mom's who had lost daughters the year my spirit brother died. Several ceremonies later, we were low on incense but still had no bride. Then, my girlfriend hesitantly spoke up.

"I had a sister who died about that same year."

"Yes! This is wonderful!" my mom said. "Let's do the Incense Burning Ceremony right now!" Mom had already adopted Michelle into our family, why not the sister as well?

"I'm sure she won't mind," Michelle said. "But I'd like to at least ask my mom for permission."

During their brief phone conversation, Michelle's mom didn't seem to think that this was unusual and gave her blessing. When we ignited the sticks of incense, they burned evenly all the way down to the end. The match with Michelle's sister had pleased the deity gods!

With a happy little smile, Mom handed Michelle a very long list. "These are the additional items necessary for the ceremony," she said.

"What ceremony?"

"The *Minghun*, the Ghost Wedding."

"Why do you want us to get these items?" I asked, looking at the paper in Michelle's hand. Some of the items could be pricey, but they all carried some spiritual or traditional significance.

"The family of the bride pays for everything," Mom said.

Michelle scowled and walked out of the room. I followed and found her with her arms folded across her chest, looking very unhappy.

"What's wrong?" I asked.

"I didn't know spending money for a Chinese Ghost Wedding was part of the bargain!" I thought that she might begin regretting having offered her sister's spirit for the marriage. Despite the cost, it seemed important to get through this for Henry's sake, and we really did want to make Mom happy. But I needed to find out what Michelle was thinking about this. After hearing her side, I saw it from her perspective. She hadn't really understood the financial ramifications of volunteering her sister, or what her part would be, because this wasn't her culture. She'd been blindsided by the sudden responsibility of "the family of the bride." I explained how important this was to my mom and to Henry. She finally softened and agreed to do it, but she wasn't very happy about it. I suggested we try to have fun and make the most of it.

Two of the items listed were a red dress and an old-fashioned, red umbrella. Because there are lots of positive attributes associated with red, such as fertility, honor, loyalty, and love—brides wear a red dress. Chinese folklore states that if a bride walks under a red umbrella whenever she is outside on her wedding day, this will ensure her protection and safety.

We needed to find an armchair with which to lay out the dress, more incense, ancestor money to burn, and also food for the deity gods. Michelle and I drove to one of the cheapest shopping places in town to get some of the items. As we were running into the store, the sky split open, and the rain began to pour. It seemed to be just one more thing intended to dampen our spirits. Michelle was still unhappy with the arrangement of having to pay for the bride's share.

We decided to shop separately; I went one direction, and she went the other. In the women's department, I found a very beautiful red dress with a Mandarin collar that seemed perfect. I looked for Michelle and saw her coming toward me with something in her hand. She held a red dress as well, but hers had come from the baby department.

"What are you doing with that?" I asked.

"Well, she died as a baby."

"But in spirit life she's an adult now." I watched as the realization hit Michelle, and slowly a smile broke across her face. Then we both laughed until our cheeks hurt. Thankfully, it broke the tension between us.

What made this all the more interesting is that the deceased brother would be the first to have a traditional Chinese style wedding. Neither of my older brothers had done so, I had not been married, and neither had Michelle. I had attended a Chinese wedding when I

was a child, but what I mostly remembered was all the delicious food. Michelle had not been part of a Ghost Wedding before and didn't hold the deceased and their afterlife with the same view I did. The people of my culture believe that the departed continues to live a life in the spirit realm. I believe my ancestors are alive and well on the other side of a non-physical divide. Sometimes smiling, sometimes steering me, but always watching over me. Maybe Michelle didn't understand the importance of such beliefs and how they connected me to my culture. It helps me keep my ancestors and my heritage close. We left that store and drove to the Chinese market and bought the rest of the items on the list.

A Ghost Wedding shares some of the more common practices that usually surround traditional Chinese weddings, and interestingly enough, a few practices from their funerals as well. Part of the ceremony requires standing at the family altar and paying respects to nature, family ancestors, and the deities. The double happiness symbol is one of the main decorations at Chinese weddings. Red and gold are often used together at weddings because the colors are said to divert negative energy. Many Chinese wedding dresses use gold thread or other gold embellishments to decorate the wedding gown.

The Tea Ceremony is performed by the bride and groom, who serve their grandparents, parents, and other members of the family while kneeling on pillows. This is done as a sign of their respect. According to Asian tradition, the family considers the couple to be married at this point. Afterward, the grandparents and parents give the bride and groom *hong bao* (lucky red envelopes). These are filled with money or jewelry and are how families gift the newlyweds.

Touching oranges wrapped in red paper and served on a red plate is believed to bring luck and prosperity to the couple, so we had them available. The Twelve Gifts are for the bride's family on the wedding day. Simplified modern weddings usually just do the essential six gifts: wedding cookies, traditional Chinese cake, candles and firecrackers, money, gold jewelry, and clothing; all of which must contain *hong bao*. And usually, gold jewelry is given to the bride. Tossing the fan is another custom that takes place before heading to the groom's house, symbolizing that the bride is tossing away her girlish past and bad habits. The tradition of fire-crackers and Lion Dancers, while entertaining, are believed to fend off evil spirits, ensuring a long, happy marriage. In the Chinese tradition, there would normally be a large wedding banquet with a cold platter of deeply symbolic foods to represent prosperity and happiness, such as bean curd, jellyfish, five-spice beef shank, pork slices, and seaweed. Hot foods would each have a symbolic meaning also: a whole fish, scallops, abalone and sea cucumber, roast suckling pig, dragon shrimp, roasted duck, and noodles in long strands for longevity, or rice which signifies abundance. Serving rice balls or yam pudding signifies the sweetness of life, and sweet lotus seeds symbolize a wish for many children.

A Ghost Wedding ceremony is slightly different, as the bride and groom are both deceased. What we did was create paper effigies that symbolized the many gifts they would have received, then we burned them, turning them into smoke which effectively releases them to the spirit world where they can be used by the newlyweds. Although our bride and groom would be unseen, appeasing deity gods required certain foods in order to favor the marriage. Fortunately, the banquet and guests were unnecessary, which meant preparing and providing considerably less food. On the day of the wedding, Michelle, my sister-in-law, my niece, and I arranged all the items for the wedding while Mom watched. She had supplied the three deity gods, representing long life, knowledge, and overall prosperity, which stood on the altar mantle. The banquet foods were placed in front of them.

At Mom's house, the dress was laid out on a chair with the red wooden umbrella next to a chair for the groom. We hung double happiness symbols all over the family room. The gifts and money were represented by paper images to be burned at the proper time (similar to what is done at funerals). As the incense burned in a pot, Mom approved of the wedding set-up and the food arrangement, all of which had only taken a few days to pull together. We had done this as a labor of love for Mom. So, I was confused that just as we were to begin, my mom stuck her arms in the sleeves of her coat as if to leave.

"We're getting ready to start . . . where are you going?" I asked.

"I don't believe in this stuff—I'm Catholic!" Then she got in her car and left.

This convenient belief in Catholicism juxtaposed with Asian culture was one of the reasons that my mom and I sometimes clashed. The culture was very ingrained in her, and what I might call superstition, she called our heritage. She wanted me to accept the beliefs that she knew and what she related to. But what I saw was that she held on to these ideas only when it was handy for her. In this way, she was doing all she could for her son, even if something wouldn't let her participate in the ceremony. I guess she just wanted to cover all her bases.

The whole ceremony took less than half an hour. Meanwhile, Mom circled the block, waiting for us to get to the part that we had to do outside on the front porch, which was burning the ancestor money in a Folger's coffee can in the dead of winter. I thought that was the longest part because the money didn't want to catch, and it was so cold. She watched us while slowly driving by and returned when we finished.

After a couple weeks there was evidence that my brother's luck did indeed change. Henry got a job and moved out of my mom's house. A few weeks later he was in a relationship with a woman and seemed to be in a happier place. My mother was elated. I hoped that everything in the afterlife would continue holding together. "If there is to be a divorce in the spirit world," I said later, "I will not be doing any of the divorce rituals for them."

Chapter 15

The Longest Hours of My Life

"I am not the product of my circumstances.
I am the product of my decisions."
~ Stephen Covey

When Mom came to America with Dad and us kids to live and start a new life, she left behind her sister Mae and her brother David in Hong Kong. Mom had a very close relationship with them. She couldn't visit China as often as she liked, but she always made a point to visit Uncle David, Aunt Mae, and their families when she did. When she got the news of her brother's death, in July 1997, it was a very sad day for our family. Mom had once shared that when the Japanese invaded Hong Kong, she carried Uncle David on her back for several miles to escape them. But her mother was assaulted by the Japanese soldiers. After that, Grandmother ended up carrying a pistol on each hip for protection. Mom and her family had been through a lot, and they were very close to each other. As soon as I heard the news about my uncle's passing, I went to Mom's house to express my condolences.

With red-rimmed eyes, she made urgent plans to travel back to China. In some ways, she seemed more affected by Uncle David's death than Dad's. But with my father's passing, she didn't need to make travel arrangements, or find her passport, or decide which clothes to pack. My mom was in her mid-sixties and the idea of her traveling almost 8,000 miles alone in a state of grief didn't seem like a great idea. Obviously, as the executor of his estate, she was obligated to go. While she waded through a long history of memories, considered which items to pack, and forgot to eat, I asked questions and offered my support.

"Mom, do you want me to fly with you to attend the funeral?"

"That is not necessary," she said, brushing imaginary lint from a dark-colored blouse. "I know your new school is keeping you very busy. However, I do want Henry to come with me."

She folded the blouse and tucked it in the suitcase lying open on the bed. Most likely she wanted to keep an eye on her youngest son. Although Henry had said he would go with her, it may have seemed to her that he was in fact blowing her off so he could go about his unseemly activities. Mom seemed worried he wouldn't follow through on his promise. She pulled a cigarette from a pack on the nightstand and lit it, inhaling sharply. She folded one arm across her body and rested her elbow on it. Exhaling a blue plume of smoke, she stared at the clothes in her closet. The hand holding her cigarette was shaking. The ashtray on the nightstand was nearly full of butts. As a two-pack-a-day smoker, she had never wanted to quit. I remembered a time when she'd had a health scare and had been rushed to the hospital. All of us kids had been in her room when the doctor came in and asked the details of her smoking habit.

"I quit smoking," she told the doctor.

"Mom!" we all said in unison.

The doctor gave us a look and turned back to her. "When did you stop smoking, Nora?"

"Yesterday," she replied.

I don't know what she had hoped to get out of telling him that little lie. A clean bill of health? Possibly she hoped to dodge the doctor's questions and inevitable lecture on the dangers of smoking and being pressured to quit. She was in the hospital, so she must have believed something wasn't right that needed immediate attention. But apparently her worst fear had not been realized and she was in no mood for the doctor's invasive queries. Once she returned safely home, she promptly resumed her toxic habit. And now, while selecting which clothes to take and cigarette haze clouding the room, she looked even more faded and fragile than the last time I'd seen her. At the time, I couldn't pinpoint why.

Flight arrangements had been made, and Mom's tickets were purchased and being held at check-in. For Henry to make the flight there were certain things he needed to do; one of them had to do with his passport. As observant as Mom was, certainly it hadn't gotten by her that he had been showing classic signs of having returned to his old ways, saying one thing and doing another. Despite the wedding ceremony we had performed for my spirit brother, Henry's good luck had not held. (It seems that the dead spirit son may have gotten divorced.) The result was that Henry had gotten even more deeply involved with drugs. His life was again in turmoil, which only made her worry all the more. And in this moment, that was the last thing she needed.

On the day of my mother's flight, I drove to the airport and Shelly came along. We tried to console Mom, but she seemed distraught and not herself. I attributed her behavior to being shocked and grief-stricken that her younger sibling had passed so suddenly, and that she was agitated at the prospect of going to China and enduring the flight alone. Shelly had been staying with her and probably understood her almost as well as I did, if not better. While we all sat at the departure gate, waiting for them to announce boarding, Mom scanned the crowds for Henry's face as travelers skirted past us with their carry-ons.

Mom looked so tiny, older, and immensely sad. I couldn't remember seeing her quite this way before. I knew she was still hoping that Henry would show, but I sensed that she knew deep down that he wasn't going to. I could almost sense how much that hurt her. In her hour of need, the one person she most wanted with her was her youngest son. The one chance for him to redeem himself for all he had put her through, and all she had done for him. And he let her down.

"I'm afraid that none of my kids will burn incense for me at the ancestral temple when it's my turn to die," she said quietly and began to cry. As I hugged my mom, I felt my throat constrict and my eyes began to fill. I could almost feel her heart breaking in my own chest.

"Oh, Mom. Don't talk that way," I said, trying to calm her concerns. I looked at her face and saw so much sorrow and disappointment there. I wanted to erase all the hurt. I wanted to make her worries melt away like ice in a heat wave. But all I could do was sit next to her and be there for her, sharing the weight of her pain. I felt sure that Uncle David's death was forcing her to look at her own mortality. Although I imagined her passing to be many years in the future, I understood her concern. She and my older brothers weren't getting along, and now she probably wondered if her youngest son was about to disappoint her as well. And unless she asked me, I had no immediate plans to go back to China.

As Mom predicted, Henry did not get it together. After last call, Mom boarded the plane alone. My niece commented that my mother had not taken any of her medications along. Shelly also shared with me that my mother—who had always taken such care with her appearance and was always the picture of elegance— had not put on her makeup or been to the hairdresser to get her hair done. Her hair! That was what had been different, what I couldn't put my finger on, and why she looked older. Mom's lack of attention to those things did not bode well.

To a point, I tried to keep track of what my mom's schedule was, when she landed, and when the funeral would be. But as I went to work, I was absorbed by the responsibilities and social niceties of running the school. Then, on the day of Uncle David's funeral, I received a call from my cousin Larry in Hong Kong. "I'm concerned about your mother. She's talking but not making any sense."

"Get her to the hospital! She's possibly suffering a stroke," I said.

"This may be a problem," he said. "Since she is no longer a citizen of Hong Kong, to admit her would cost about $48,000."

"Don't wait! I'll have the money wired there, and I'll take the next plane out." I quickly filled Michelle in and left her in charge. I rushed home to pack appropriate clothes. A flurry of phone calls ensued: wiring money to Hong Kong, discussing direct flight availabilities, purchasing plane tickets and other arrangements. I felt as if someone had pressed a "go" button, and my day was spent hurdling one obstacle after another. Everything seemed speeded up and urgent. The stress was further intensified by Mom's life hanging in the balance. The first opportunity to think about what it meant that my mother was in the hospital came after the wheels left the ground in Ohio and I was in the air heading for China.

The next seventeen hours were the longest of my whole life. My mom was elderly and already distraught about Henry and, now, Uncle David's final wishes. After a number of heart attacks, she'd had a stent installed. On top of that, she was a chain smoker. All these together made her situation that much more precarious. That my relatives had caught Mom's symptoms early was in her favor. Wiring money to the hospital so they would admit her, another plus. She would be getting proper care while I was in flight. I really hoped these things would buy me enough time to get there in case . . . I didn't want to think about that just then.

My thoughts see-sawed between best and worst-case scenarios. When I felt myself starting to get emotional, I pushed it aside. Until I had all the facts, I didn't need to go there, not unless and until something dire really happened. I wanted to believe that I would see her again, propped up in a hospital bed complaining about the food, maybe even the staff, with her sister and brother-in-law at her bedside. I wanted to believe that she'd been admitted in time to prevent permanent brain damage and paralysis. I tried to imagine the look that would be on her face when she saw me step into her room, and that she'd be happy that I had rushed halfway around the world to be with her. I held on to that idea the most, picturing every detail so that I could form it into reality. The thought that troubled me like an annoying, circling bee was her statement that it was not necessary for me to fly with her to Hong Kong. I wished that I had bought the ticket anyway.

A memory crept into my mind of when my grandmother, Mom's mother, passed away. She was in Hong Kong; we were in Columbus. The family held the funeral in China, but my mom couldn't go. They sent her pictures, which isn't the same. The photos showed an open casket. There were a lot of mourners, family and friends, gathered together. Custom dictates burning a lot of incense, Chinese money, joss sticks, and many effigies of items that the deceased will need in the afterlife. There is the tray of certain foods: oranges, a bowl of rice, pork, and some sweets, which I remember seeing on a tray, sitting on the coffin. I remember Mom explaining the parts of the funeral, what they symbolized and the importance of each.

As I counted down the hours to landing, I recognized the butterflies in my stomach and worked at maintaining a sense of calm as I had been trained in martial arts. I tried to meditate. I visualized sending healing energy to her. I wanted to focus on good thoughts and believe that she would come through this; I imagined assisting her with settling Uncle David's affairs and accounts and then bringing her back home. I wanted to believe that we would have many more conversations together—even the ones that exasperated me. I tried to visualize many more trips to China under better circumstances. It seemed obvious that it was now necessary to have the "final wishes" conversation. Aside from having incense burned on her behalf at the ancestor's temple, I really didn't know what she wanted.

Though the flight was long, it was uneventful, and I slept through part of it. When the plane landed in Hong Kong, I looked for Aunt Mae, Uncle Mike, and my two cousins, Larry and Bobby, who were in the airport waiting to greet me. Hong Kong is normally crowded, and the masses of people seemed even larger that day.

"You're late," my aunt said, her mouth downturned.

"The plane was not late, and I am on time." I smiled, hoping to keep things light.

"No, I didn't mean late with the plane; I meant about your mom," she said. "Too late. She passed away."

What? Mom! I felt my breath catch in my throat and the numbness was almost immediate. I just stood there in stunned silence. Aunt Mae tied a piece of black cloth on my arm, an outward indication that I was in mourning. I tried to let the words penetrate my brain. Crowds of people spiraled around me, and I thought for a moment that I would fall. *My mother is gone.* I felt alone in my soul, an American in China who barely knows the language. The only people who can help are at least as distraught as I am.

My aunt was very stoic. She told me that, before taking my mother to the hospital, she had found her Hong Kong ID in her purse. They admitted Mom under her maiden name, Tsang. In my shock I barely heard Aunt Mae say that they had notified Michelle. She was already flying to Hong Kong to meet me. I was almost too numb to be grateful for that bit of news.

Thick, smiling crowds jostled us, called out to one another, and lines were longer than I recalled from previous trips. Why were the people surrounding us smiling and cheering and silly with excitement? The strange air of festivity swirling around us felt garish, and completely out of synch given my circumstances. What was going on? I wondered if the unexpected loss of my mother had magnified my perception. *My mom is gone. My mom has died. This can't be true!* I only half heard my cousin Larry explaining that it had been very difficult to find a room on such short notice. All the hotels were booked solid because of "the celebration."

"What celebration?" I asked.

"The hundred-year lease to the British is over, and Hong Kong is being returned to China!" The Chinese people, and Hong Kongers in particular, were making a big deal of this momentous occasion. It looked as though one billion Chinese had come to Hong Kong to celebrate. As we pressed through the throngs, it felt like we were the only ones in all of China who were mourning. Despite the hordes of people who had descended upon the city, Larry had managed to find very nice accommodation. Luckily—and because he knew someone in hospitality—he was able to book a room for me at a five-star hotel that first night. Given the circumstances, I should have been more grateful for the room. But I could hardly enjoy it.

As I looked at the lights of Hong Kong, the thought that I had missed my mother's last moments broke my heart. To stem the tide of tears, I considered how lucky I had been to have developed a good relationship with her over the last ten years. I had come to appreciate her and was glad for the time we had shared. I wasn't ready for it to be over. Despite having few regrets, my soul had already begun to ache in response to the loss. The list of things that I would miss about her had begun to lengthen. Exhausted from the flight and the unhappy news, getting some sleep seemed like the best idea. I hoped a few hours rest would help me collect my thoughts and strengthen me for the days ahead. And if not, at least Michelle would arrive soon, and, somehow, she would help me get through this.

Chapter 16

Bill Mitchell was Right

Michelle's flight was scheduled to arrive late at night, and my aunt's family and I went back to the airport to pick her up. Her presence would be a huge comfort. At the airport, we stood in queues still thickly crowded with people. When we finally found Michelle, she tried to speak but seemed tongue-tied and had a strange look on her face. "I thought . . . I don't know, I'm confused."

"What?" I asked.

"I saw your mom," she said. "I saw her smiling at me and waving to me. Just before I saw you."

"What?"

"Your mom was waving to me from the crowd."

"No," I said, "that was not . . ."

"I know it was her," Michelle said.

She knew if that were the case, she wouldn't be in Hong Kong just then. Maybe she had seen a very real-looking ghost of my mother. It was very strange, and she couldn't explain it.

Even though I would have preferred staying in the luxury hotel, because of the massive citywide celebration, all the five-star accommodation had previously been reserved. Larry happened to find us another room in a different hotel. Before we got into the room, we noticed there was a lot of housekeeping going on even though it was very late. While Michelle and I were in our room, we noticed that housekeeping occurred at every hour. We didn't think much about it until we turned on the television and saw porn on every station. We were in a brothel!

Luckily, Larry got another hotel for the rest of our two-week stay. During most of that time, I kept busy dealing with funeral arrangements for my mom. When a relative passes away in another country, everything is automatically more complicated. One step of the process is that whoever identifies the body becomes responsible for carrying out the last wishes and makes the decision regarding the remains. As her daughter, the first step was to identify Mom's body. Michelle and I were taken to the hospital. At reception we stated that we had come to identify Nora Tsang, and I was so overcome all I could do was cry, too emotional to even consider the task. "I'll do it," Michelle volunteered.

She followed an attendant to the viewing room and was gone for a short time. When she returned, she looked a little shaken. I think it was almost as upsetting for her as it was for me. "That is your mom." She had much more to say, but she didn't tell me then, because I was already devastated.

Then there was a complication. Mom had not been admitted under her married name "Yee" which was the same as mine, but under her maiden name "Tsang." As a result, they refused to release her body to me. I spent a lot of time trying to convince them and prove that Nora was my mom who lived in America. They saw her as their Hong Kong citizen. We went around and around. They held all the cards; I was powerless. It seemed we had reached an impasse. I didn't know what more to do. Utterly and completely frustrated, I had a meltdown right there in the office. Finally, one guy felt sorry for me and signed the release. I guess they didn't think anyone but a relative would be that upset. With that issue finally resolved, we decided the funeral and burial would take place in China, and then we would hold a memorial service in Ohio for her family and friends.

In the meantime, there were many decisions to be made. While making arrangements for Mom and settling Uncle David's estate,

I heard many stories from my relatives about those who had transitioned to the spirit world, starting with my mom. My aunt had shared some of my mom's history that I had never heard. Though I had noticed that Mom always had a fantastic physique, Aunt Mae said Mom was beautiful and thin enough to have been a model. All kinds of young men wanted to date her and court her. And I found it ironic that her only daughter didn't want anything to do with any of those beautification practices. I didn't want my hair styled, to wear jewelry, makeup, or dresses—I was a tomboy. According to my aunt, and against cultural belief, my mother had insisted on sleeping in my uncle's place. This is never to be done because it is widely understood that ancestral spirits come for the spirit of the deceased. My relatives tried to talk my mom out of it, but my mom told her sister she did not believe in this. The next day, Mom reported with wide eyes that she had felt somebody tugging on her toe in the middle of the night, which made a believer out of her.

Though I enjoyed hearing these stories, the days were filled with many details and a seemingly never-ending stream of decisions. In midst of these exhausting responsibilities, Tom and my sister-in-law phoned. They wanted to notify me about Henry's recent shameful activities. He'd broken into Mom's place, taken her and my uncle's checks, forged their signatures, and cashed them. He'd stolen Mom's credit cards, which he used all over town. "And now," they said, "a detective is looking for him."

"Just change the locks on the door," I said, too overwhelmed and too far away to be of much help. Dealing with Henry's mess would have to wait until my return. I was glad that Mom hadn't seen how he had taken advantage of this tragedy. "And don't let him back into Mom's place!"

I learned a lot about my family while in Hong Kong, and at the end of two very daunting weeks, my Uncle Mike made an announcement.

"I would like to treat you and Michelle to a fun day out. You have two choices. You can go see the largest Buddha in the world," he suggested glumly. Then he suddenly smiled with big eyes and switched to an animated voice. "Or we can go take a tour of the brand new airport!"

He seemed very excited about the latter, and I really didn't care. Although a break sounded like a wonderful idea. We elected to tour Hong Kong's enormous new airport at Chek Lap Kok. Uncle arranged a tour guide to come and pick us up. My aunt stayed home, but he, Michelle, and I left for our destination. The airport was huge and the construction of it was an impressive feat because it had been built on land reclaimed from the sea. Although the airport was ultra-modern and beautiful as airports go, my thoughts were still preoccupied with Mom. She would never come here to visit again. She would never see her own house again. Trying to convince myself that she was gone proved not only difficult, but painful. I was effectively an orphan.

I tried to console myself with the idea that she was at peace. That she had no more worries, she wasn't alone, and she was with my father, one of her sons, her brother, and many relatives. I tried to keep in the forefront of my mind that she would be watching over me from the other side. While we drove to our destination, I thought of the strange conversations that we'd had and the silly and weird things we'd fought over. Like her commenting on the sun one night, when really it was a beautiful full moon in an early twilight sky. And then there was the day Mom came home with the most incredible story about a man she had seen.

"I saw a man, and he only had a head."

I looked at her and waited for her to say more. Instead, she took out her cigarettes, put one in her mouth and lit it. She tossed the pack on the kitchen counter. "Mom, what do you mean that he was just a head?"

"Yeah, he was just a head."

"He can't be just a head! Did he not have arms and legs?"

"No! He was just a head." She repeated and flicked her ashes in a metal ashtray and gave me a hard look.

"He can't just be a head, Mom," I said. I could tell she was getting annoyed. She took a puff on her cigarette, eyeing me the way she did when I disagreed with her. But I pushed it anyway. "Mom? What do you mean?"

She exhaled before answering me. "Today I saw a man without a body."

"What do you mean he didn't have a body? He has to have a body!"

"No! He only had a head!" she insisted.

"Well first of all, Mom, he has to have a heart and lungs to breathe." I was coming at it from a practical standpoint. Maybe a part of me was worried that her mind was starting to slip, or she was having a drug interaction hallucination. Because she couldn't or wouldn't explain to me in a way that made sense, it escalated into an argument. You know what it's like when two people believe with all their heart that they're the only one who's right. She just got mad and gave up on me; she held up her hand and waved me off, meaning she's done. She stubbed out her cigarette and walked out of the room with a cloud of smoke lingering where she had been.

"What? Come on!" I said, frustrated. I wanted to understand what was going on with her. She wouldn't talk about it anymore. Now that she was gone, I wondered if I would ever understand what she really saw.

As we finished our tour of the airport, the guide announced that the bus would make another stop, somewhere along the road. There weren't many of us: the guide, the driver, my uncle, me and Michelle, and maybe one other stranger. The guide wanted to stop at a site called a *hutong*, in an area where ancient villages were located. A *hutong* is a narrow street or alleyway in an old residential section of a Chinese city. Many *hutongs* have lasted for centuries.

Once we arrived, we got out to look around. As we walked through the tiny alley, I noticed huge black-and-white photos of three women hung above an altar area. The tour guide spoke in Cantonese, which I didn't understand, and I was only half-listening. My uncle looked very excited as she related the history of this particular *hutong*. Then, my uncle came running toward me and Michelle.

"Helen, you're not going to believe this! This *hutong* belonged to the family of Tsang—which is your mom's maiden name!" my uncle said. "This *hutong* was the village of Tsang and belonged to your ancestors at one time. The women in the photos are your ancestors!"

"What?! Really? That is so cool!" I was more than a bit shocked that we'd "randomly" landed here. Suddenly, I felt the presence of my mom. It was as though she was saying, "Hey, you found me!" I allowed myself to be enveloped in it, to feel her fully. While it lasted, the feeling was similar to being embraced and held. I wanted that to last forever. Still raw from the sudden loss, tears ran down my face. I wasn't ready for her to be gone. I didn't want her to go. There were a million things I was going to miss about her. I had already been cheated out of the chance to tell her goodbye in person before she died. I wanted to be able to tell her goodbye in some meaningful way. I couldn't think of what that would be. But just then, I didn't feel alone. I felt that she understood. I believed that she knew that I had made the trip for her, and her presence felt like an acknowledgement of that. It was difficult to leave that place—I wanted that feeling to stay with me. However, the guide insisted on making one last "random" stop. As we traveled to the next place, I felt that the essence of my mother remained with me, guiding us along, leading us to the next destination.

Then the bus stopped in front of the ancestor temple! This was one of the last things she mentioned to me before boarding the plane. I knew this ancient ritual was important and culturally significant to her. Her presence was so strong that if I closed my eyes I could almost believe she was standing next to me, and it was deeply meaningful and emotional to my very core. I was able to fulfill my mother's final wish, to burn incense for her in the traditional Chinese custom. I knew in my heart that all my relatives in the afterlife had escorted us to that place so that I would not miss the opportunity to burn incense for my mom, as well as my uncle, and my ancestors. In the Chinese tradition, incense is burned to help make the space sacred, avert bad luck, commemorate funerals, for daily prayers, and to pay respect to ancestors. In that private moment of ritual, I felt that she was at peace knowing one of her kids had honored her in the place and in the way that she would have wanted. It was a moment in which I could almost touch the other side, a moment that connected me to her; and whatever veil separated us was so thin that I could feel Mom's love. It must have pleased her that I had not lost touch with my heritage after all. It was an important moment that I felt was shared by both of us.

The additional stops had not been planned by us, Uncle had nothing to do with them, and I hardly had the presence of mind to plan anything under the weight of Mom's death. It was just so surreal how everything had lined up.

After that excursion, it was time to go back to Columbus. Michelle and I boarded the plane to return home. "Bill Mitchell was right," she said.

As her words sank in, I recalled a shared evening out from six months earlier. Michelle and I had gone to an event that hosted a psychic named Bill Mitchell. He had selected people from the audience and gave them short "readings" in which he briefly described events that had occurred or would occur in the person's life. It was entertaining, but we had no way of ever finding out the rest of the story. And then he looked at me. "You are going to learn much about your family's ancestors and heritage this year." I was surprised that he had singled me out and wasn't sure I could trust what he said. I may have even laughed it off as "woo-woo stuff." The truth is that Mom didn't really share a whole lot and wasn't that talkative about her family back home. I knew for me to learn about my ancestors I would have to go back to Hong Kong. That was the only way to learn more.

At the end of that event, it was still on my mind. As we were leaving, I wanted to put Michelle's mind at ease, and maybe even my own. "What he said is never going to happen," I said, knowing what it would require. "Because I'm not planning on returning to Hong Kong."

How wrong I had been. Although I was surprised by how the events transpired months later, I was very appreciative of all that had unfolded on this journey: for my mom's return home, to feeling her presence at the *hutong* and burning incense. As the plane took off, I looked out the window one last time. All the sunny days, from the time of my arrival to my departure, were coming with us, just as the billowing black clouds of monsoon season were returning to the harbor. I should have realized even then that this was not the end of the story.

Chapter 17

The Last Word

Henry and I had not crossed paths since my return to Columbus, a decade before. He was deeply into a bad scene, freebasing cocaine and using other hardcore stuff. I heard snippets of conversation regarding the trouble he always seemed to find himself in. And I knew he was keeping bad company and living dangerously close to the edge. Because I hadn't seen him or spent any time with him, I had not observed how profoundly he had changed, or the destruction that drugs had caused in him.

When he didn't show up at the airport to travel with Mom, I was disappointed for her. I was annoyed with Henry for letting her down. Even though he had become unreliable, it didn't occur to me that he had been planning to take advantage of Mom's absence. I didn't know until I got back from China that Henry had stayed at a Holiday Inn for a month doing all kinds of crazy stuff and living it up with his friends, because he had access to all of Mom's money.

When I finally spoke with the detective, it made me sad to think how much my grandfathers, grandmothers, and parents had sacrificed so that we could have a good life here in America. None of us had control over Henry nor could we prevent him from wasting his opportunity to succeed, or his very life. I was never mad at him. I resented the life he chose to live, for stealing from and disrespecting our mom, and for shaming our family. In spite of my feelings, he was still my brother. I called him to provide him with the date and time of Mom's memorial.

"I'm not going," he said.

"Well, I'm not trying to judge you. If you don't come, I don't really care," I said. I was already done with him. "This is it, Henry. I think, honestly, you're going to have regrets all your life if you don't come. So, you have the information. Come if you want. I'm not forcing you." I left it up to him to decide. I had a million other things to do.

At the memorial, all my mom's friends came to pay their final respects. It was in conversations with these friends that I heard more stories about her and learned more about my family. Soon I was hearing about dreams and other strange things in a conversation with Mom's best friend, Elaine.

"Your mom came to me in a dream," she said. "The weird thing was your mom didn't look like your mom."

"What do you mean?" I asked.

"She had gray hair." I could tell Elaine thought this carried significant importance. She certainly knew how meticulous Mom was about the way she looked. She always presented herself as very classy and elegant and consistently made sure her hair was dyed black. "In the dream, she had gray-white hair and something in her mouth!"

"Holy shit!" I said, shocked. I hadn't told anyone about Mom's hair. This lined up with what Shelly had told me the day we'd taken her to the airport. What struck me as strange was Elaine saying she had seen something in Mom's mouth. According to Chinese folklore, various things can be placed in the mouth of the departed, all of which carry symbolic meaning and are designed to help them in their afterlife. A pearl is believed to protect the deceased, a coin is to pay guardian spirits, and grains of rice are believed to guarantee the loved one will have enough to eat. However, I later learned that cloth or cotton can be put in the mouth to fill out gaunt looking cheeks. This is done for the sake of the family who must identify them, or who will be viewing them for the last time. While it sounded strange and unlikely, Elaine's dream caused me to question a lot of other details having to do with Mom's passing. For example: even though Mom was on a whole bunch of different prescriptions for her heart, why had she not taken them with her? Why hadn't she attended to her hair? The answer seemed obvious to me: she'd had a premonition of her own death.

While I talked with some of my mom's friends, my back was toward the entrance of the room. Suddenly, all my mom's friends gasped aloud at the same time, and the room went dead silent. They were all looking past me, to the door. I was like, "Oh my God! What's going on?" I turned around. And I gasped too! There in the doorway stood my youngest brother, Henry.

I stared because the drugs had turned him into a walking skeleton, and he looked terrible. And while his physical appearance was shocking, the guest gasped because he was wearing a red shirt! Red is associated with good luck and happiness, great for a wedding. But at a Chinese funeral, it's bad luck.

He didn't know what to do once he was in the room, so I walked over to him. "I'm glad you came," I said.

"I thought I was supposed to wear red. No one else is wearing red . . ."

"Dark colors for funerals."

"Oh, man. I'm sorry . . . I didn't remember that."

I didn't give him a hard time. Maybe he'd heard about the Ghost Wedding ceremony we did on his behalf and mixed up what was appropriate for funerals and weddings. Who knew his state of mind? Wearing a red shirt said more about his being out of touch with his culture. Certainly, it was not his intent to be disrespectful. He would never have chosen to embarrass himself that way. I was glad that he bothered to show up at all. It was the best he could do to even show his face. He quickly paid his respects and didn't stay long. It was the last time I saw Henry alive.

After I got home, Michelle and I were talking, and I shared with her Elaine's dream and that she had seen my mom with gray hair, and that she'd said Mom had something white in her mouth.

"Oh my God!" Michelle said.

"What?"

"I forgot to tell you. When I identified your mom, there was a piece of white cloth in her mouth."

It gave me the chills that Michelle had seen what Elaine had seen in her dream. Maybe Michelle didn't remember because she thought I would have known about the cloth, or, possibly, that it would upset me further.

Even after that, strange things continued to happen. A few months after Mom's death, I was driving down High Street to the Short North. All of a sudden, I saw something coming towards me. This man was rolling along on a cart that was gurney-height—eye-level if you're sitting in a car. As he's coming towards me, all I can see is his head! He was lying belly down and didn't have any appendages—no arms, no legs—and was navigating this customized cart with a joystick in his mouth. While I'm staring (and trying to drive without causing an accident) I remember thinking, *Oh my God, she was right! This is the person Mom saw.* A part of me believes that she orchestrated this sighting so she could win this argument. I took it as a sign from her that she was still communicating with me, and that she finally had the last word. I could almost hear her saying, "See? I told you so!"

I wasn't the only one who was still thinking about her. In the year following her death, my oldest brother Tom came to realize that he hadn't treated Mom very well at the end of her years. By that point, Mom needed money. She owned two homes, next to each other, one of which used to be my grandfather's. She lived in one and Tom stayed in the other with his family. However, he paid no money to Mom for rent. She had been living on the principle of the inheritance from my grandfather. But it was running out. When she asked Tom for money, he got mad and held a grudge against her. He kept the grandkids from visiting her, even though she lived right next door. This hurt Shelly, too, because she was very close to Mom. Later, Tom was very troubled by guilt and regret. Somehow, he and Elaine ended up talking, and he told her all of this.

"This is what you can do to pay respects to your mom, for treating her so badly," Elaine said. She spelled out a solution to appease his guilty conscience. "Find a picture of her and go to the biggest body of water nearby . . ."

Tom went to either Hoover Dam or Alum Creek. Following Elaine's instructions to the letter, he held Mom's picture above his head. He said three things aloud, like, "Mom, I'm sorry for not treating you better. Please forgive me. I love you." The fact that he did the ritual impressed upon me how guilty he felt because my brother was an atheist.

Since none of my brothers treated Mom very well, I guarded her estate jealously. My attitude toward them was like, "I dare you to try and contest Mom's will or anything that belonged to her." Mom owned a lot of very expensive jewelry. In the end, I gave my niece Shelly several pieces to remember Mom by because they had been very close.

On top of grieving Mom and Uncle David, speaking to an estate attorney, managing the closing of Mom's estate, arranging for her memorial in Ohio, and dealing with Henry's bad behavior, I was still responsible for running my share of a growing business. If Michelle and I ever questioned whether we had chosen the right business model, being away for several weeks had been the acid test. We were pleased and relieved to find the building still standing, and our staff working together like a priceless Swiss watch. And, indeed, our staff was amazing. Though we had left abruptly, they all rose to the challenge and kept the business running smoothly in our absence. I couldn't have been more grateful for each one of them and, oddly enough, to my grandfather. Throughout the entire process of building my company, I thought a lot about him and felt he was always kind of there. I had a sense that he was guiding me along. Because my grandfather ran such successful businesses, he inspired me to become an entrepreneur. Even though he was an extremely hard worker, he made a point to enjoy life when he wasn't working. He had outside interests, and I made sure I developed some too. He invested his money in property, the business, and in people, and I did the same. I watched how he interacted with his customers and employees. How he always worked at maintaining strong connections to people. He excelled in making people feel welcome and valued, that they mattered to him, and that their contribution was deeply appreciated. I wanted to emulate that and have the people around me feel what he imparted to his circle of influence. Because he made a point to treat people fairly and treat them well, they in return were incredibly loyal to him. This was true of his staff and his patrons. His integrity was obvious in business and in his life. I wanted that same loyalty. Being friendly opens a lot more doors and crosses many racial divides. In the business of hospitality and food service, a welcoming personality goes with the territory. Throughout his years in restaurants, my grandfather met all kinds of people. He was kind to all and had a smile for everyone. I saw the positive effect it had on those he interacted with. He made it look effortless.

These attributes are even more important in the sports/alternative medicine space where you are dealing one-on-one and physically touching another person's body. My business was such that massage services could be volunteered to help various groups, such as local marathons and sports events, as I mentioned earlier. But I discovered a whole new world of fun when I got interested in the larger volunteer scene.

Chapter 18

Part of Something Larger

Like many people, I lead a busy life. If I'm going to give up my precious time, it must be something that really speaks to my heart. After retiring from competing in Taekwondo, I had more time to pursue other interests. Although much of my volunteer work has been through martial arts or Asian American connections, I developed new business and personal connections through volunteer experiences. As an Asian American woman, who is lesbian and a longtime business owner, representation is very important to me. All voices are important.

I heard about Stonewall Columbus, a group focused on increasing awareness of the LGBTQ+ community. Stonewall is also a platform for fostering understanding, getting support for the LGBTQ+ community, speaking about transgender, and everything in between. I wanted to be a part of something larger that was important to me. Stonewall Columbus is one of the main organizations responsible for putting together the annual Gay Pride March, which has attracted a growing number of attendees since the early 80s—over 700,000 people in recent years! The Gay Pride March is Stonewall's biggest fundraising event of the year. This was something I could get excited about!

While volunteering at Stonewall, I met the woman who was serving as executive director. She encouraged me to become a board member with the Columbus Pride Parade. After serving on the board for a few years, I was encouraged to run for vice president of Stonewall. To my surprise, I was voted in as VP!

Stonewall sponsors a group called "The Trailblazers." They are a group of LGBTQ+ seniors to whom I currently teach Tai Chi and Qigong. It has also been great to have a venue that brings the community together. In the Stonewall Gallery, one of my favorite activities is to provide space for artists, especially lesbian artists, to present or showcase their artwork. I also got to curate my own personal exhibition, which featured many of my new paintings. On opening night, thanks to very supportive friends, I sold fifteen pieces!

My skills gained by running a business were learned through doing. It was a given that I would make mistakes; it's just part of paying your dues. As I gained experience, I tweaked, revised, and pivoted. I learned when and how to take certain risks. Having my own business forced me to do things outside of my comfort level. For example, I once had a phobia of public speaking. It's been suggested that as many as 75% of the population suffer from this anxiety. There are many ways to overcome it, but I believed in facing it head-on. In my business, there were commencement speeches to give, orientations to lead, and a myriad of speaking engagements I accepted to promote our business, teach classes, and share vital information. Out of necessity, and because I'm willing to put myself out there, I've become more skilled in public speaking. Was I afraid? Yes, at first. But again, I learned through martial arts training how to calm those butterflies. Instead of worrying about every speaking event, I learned what I needed to know to become better. I practiced, and I kept speaking in public. By doing this, my anxiety around public speaking disappeared. I would have missed many opportunities had I shied away because of that fear.

My own belief is that fear limits thinking. I have learned to do things that feel uncomfortable, even when I don't know how they will turn out. I've learned to ask, "How can I make this work?" I don't worry about failing. Instead, I envision how success will look. I don't care if I look foolish, that only lasts a moment. The gold is in the wisdom gained from trying. Opportunities can present themselves to anyone, and everyone has their own way of aligning with them. I noticed that many people are paralyzed by fear. When it comes to taking that next step, doing something new, or just different, they're not comfortable. Some are so uncomfortable that they can't move forward. One of my gifts is recognizing opportunities when they arise and quickly evaluating the risk. Wisdom is knowing when to act. Those "random" chances that appeared in my life were almost always lined up with something that I had been focusing on and thinking about. They usually benefited not only me but the people who participated with me, which in turn cascaded down to many more people; students, friends, and clients.

I realized that competing brought out my spirit of determination, and a desire to become better. If it's something I really want to do, I keep at it until I succeed. As a child interested in competitive sports and constantly challenging myself, I sometimes created my own opportunities. I enjoyed being included and being a part of a larger community. Being interested in many things as an adult presented me with opportunities in my personal, business, and spiritual life.

Through the seeds planted in my mind by my grandfather's example, I learned many lessons. He was infinitely curious and always learning. He balanced work with several enjoyable hobbies that he found fulfilling, including—as I mentioned before—playing music. He appeared to be genuinely happy and at peace in his life. The idea that he could do better than his father and grandfather had been seeded and sown in my grandfather's mind, energizing a vision and feeding a goal. Because he'd been told he was capable of achieving more, he chose to do exactly that. Relying on his excellent communication skills, he left the hard labor of farming and found a career where his gifts accelerated his business accomplishments. He was careful with his money and, while helping his family and his community through sponsorships, he became a restaurateur.

My parents were also successful and excelled with their talents. They shared them with the public. Between my parent's and my grandfather's examples, it seems I was destined for success. While that may be partly true, a lot depended on me making the right choices at critical points. There were many intersections throughout my earthly sojourn where I could have chosen differently. What if I had not tried out for sports? What if I had not taken martial arts or tried full-contact fighting? What if I had never gone to Florida or met Michelle?

Luckily for me, I had good friends to encourage me and amazing mentors who appeared at just the right moments along the way. Mentors like Master Choi, and like my dear friend Sunny whose timely words caused me to pursue fighting. Also, there was Wen Mei Yu whose instruction helped me get my vitality in order. By observing and listening to the role models around me, and constantly learning, I was provided with the insight and wisdom to choose correctly.

Along the way I learned that as dreams come to pass and goals are achieved, it's important to keep creating new ones. I still had dreams of two specific additions that I believed would really enhance our business and elevate the institute. One was a nursing program, and the other was an acupuncture program. I really wanted both, but they seemed very much out of reach for us—if not impossible. I didn't have any idea of how to make either one of them happen. Nor could I ever have orchestrated the events that would suddenly make them possible.

Chapter 19

American Institute
of Alternative Medicine

In 1999, Michelle and I planned a tour of the United Kingdom followed by a lengthy excursion to China. When we learned that one school in Texas had scheduled a China trip to explore Traditional Chinese Medicine, we decided to join them on their tour. Our school was doing well, but I had been considering additional programs, one of which included training and uses of medicinal herbs. By tagging along, we hoped to learn modalities that might be useful.

The cache of ancient wisdom to be found in China is vast, and there is no shortage of teachers willing to share their knowledge. We participated in cooking classes, learned the healing dynamics of cupping, and even experienced *gua sha* (pronounced *gwuh shah*), a non-invasive massage method which rubs or scrapes the skin's surface with rounded tools to unblock negative energy and increase blood circulation. By training with some Tai Chi and Qigong masters, I learned internal martial arts disciplines and the value of having a balance of internal and external strength. Martial arts disciplines are much more than explosive kicking and challenging your body physically. It can also improve your vitality—the Chi—the life-force energy. To do that, you must focus inward. Yoga systems and certain meditations are based on that principle.

While in China, the opportunity arose for an excursion to Tibet. Not everyone was as excited about it as me and Michelle. Some in our group were already unwell, and others worried about exposing themselves to high elevations, which often results in altitude sickness. Since we were in great shape, and willing to risk it, we added it to our itinerary. Tibet's majestic mountains and the deeply spiritual people who live there made that country one of the best places I have ever visited. The Potala Palace, also known as Buddha Mountain, is the highest castle in the world. At 12,300 feet above sea level, it once functioned as the winter home of the Dalai Lama, until he went into exile in 1957. Two years later, it became a museum and a huge tourist attraction. I was thrilled to see it as part of our tour.

The palace holds deep significance because the earthly remains of many Dalai Lamas—high-ranking monks and Buddhist teachers of the past—were laid to rest there, either in celestial burials or cremated, and their ashes kept in funeral stupas. Many Tibetan Buddhists make pilgrimages there. It is a miles-long journey during which they perform a series of specific moves which include kneeling and prostrating themselves to the ground, then rising with a salutation every few steps. This ritual is repeated in extreme reverence every inch of the path, and to gain religious merit. Prayer wheels are cylindrical devices, often found under roofed kiosks, inscribed with mantras in the Tibetan language, which can be recited on the journey. We were told pilgrim travelers heavily relied on the goodness of others to provide food for them along the way, and it counts as religious merit to give them alms.

Potala Palace consists of two parts, the Red Palace and the White Palace. To reach either one, steep steps must be climbed. The trek to the palace grounds was difficult given the altitude, but I wasn't going to let a flight of stairs come between me and seeing the rich history inside, no matter how many steps there were. While the architecture is breathtaking—one thousand rooms!—the intricate paintings, artwork, and tapestries, despite being ancient, were timelessly beautiful. It is also the home of 10,000 Buddha statues and an equal number of scroll paintings. It is quite a feat that vast amounts of relics and artwork has survived hundreds, sometimes thousands, of years.

The chanting of monks filled the air. Older monks trained younger monks via debates, in which an older monk asks a question and then claps his hands, and the answer must be given immediately. Fragrant incense burned throughout the palace, which is illuminated by yak oil candles. The distinctive musky odor didn't appeal to my senses. The monks invited us into an area outside the palace where they served us yak butter tea. Although I didn't care for it, my brave travel partner Michelle drank it . . . and suffered for it the next two days. Yak meat, which is one of the food staples in Tibet, is very tender. I was surprised that I liked the taste.

But what I found most stunning was the view from the rooftop of the world. We hiked way up into the mountain regions to Emerald Lake, a salt-water lake in Dachaidan, Haixi, Qinghai. It was of course bright green and astoundingly gorgeous. The air was very thin, but the landscape was pristine.

In Lhasa, the capital city, I learned that the Tibetan people are incredibly strong. When we arrived at the hotel, we were given rooms on the third or fourth floor. We were already feeling the effects of being at high altitude: the lack of oxygen, getting headaches, and feeling nauseous. My backpack alone was about seventy pounds, seriously heavy. And everyone in our tour group had them. The Sherpa, who was a tiny little woman my size, took all of our bags. We took the elevator. We were grateful for the respite from their weight. When the elevator doors opened, she already had all our bags in the hallway. She had arranged them on her back somehow, taken the stairs, and still got there before us! We were astonished at her strength. She was in such great shape; she wasn't even breathing hard. I really don't know how she did it.

But one more surprise awaited us. While on the China tour, one of the women with us spoke to me and Michelle. She predicted that we would successfully start an acupuncture school. That sounded great, and I wanted it to be true. Certain obstacles would have to be overcome. In Ohio, only physicians were allowed to administer acupuncture. The other downside was that, at that time, there were no schools teaching it in the entire state.

"A friend is going to introduce you to someone who will help you with that program," she said confidently.

Well, okay! I thanked her and filed it with the dreams and goals for the school. I was a little skeptical because I didn't see how it would happen. But Michelle and I decided to keep an open mind because I think she knew how much I really wanted to do it. In our travels through different parts of Asian countries, we gathered information and studied different models of clinics. We had gained a lot of great information and were excited about all we had learned. It was our hope to make alternative medicine accessible to more people, offer more therapies, and expand the school's programs.

Then came the first in a series of shocking surprises. In 2000, acupuncture was legalized as a legitimate therapy in Ohio! We were thrilled that such an enormous obstacle had been removed. Acupuncture was such a natural fit that one of our massage therapy instructors had decided to enroll in a specific four-year acupuncture certification program in 1997—even though it was in New Mexico! She moved there temporarily while her family remained in Ohio. There, she met the dean of the school, Dr. Wong. Eventually, she shared with him that she had two friends who started had a massage school in Ohio and were now interested in starting an acupuncture program there as well. Dr. Wong and his wife were not happy in New Mexico. In his excitement, he asked our staff member for more information and then surprised her.

"I'm going to Ohio to meet your two friends."

"Oh? Well, wait a minute!"

Very determined to meet us, he arrived in our building one day and introduced himself to us. "I'm Dr. Wong, the dean of the Oriental Medical School in New Mexico." He proceeded to explain his credentials and all that he knew.

As excited as we were to meet him, our therapist getting certified had been the first step in testing the waters for the program. Until that moment, it was still largely a dream. I wanted to be honest with him. "To tell you the truth," I said, "we don't have any idea how all this is going to play out."

"Well," he said, "I want to help. I've already designed the curriculum for it."

For us, that was one of the missing pieces. What were the chances that a guy from New Mexico shows up just at the right time, willing to move to our location, with all the information that we needed? It was a very cool, ethereal feeling to know that this is the person who's supposed to help us, just as the woman on our China trip predicted. We were awestruck.

In 2001 when we offered acupuncture, our newly licensed staff member taught the class. At the launch of that program, we had fourteen students—the same number that had started when we began the massage program! We took that to be a sign that it would be successful, just as the massage school had been.

Because of this significant addition, we all agreed that we needed to change up the name. We had a few more ideas for programs that would fit in this vein; it needed to be inclusive without being too specific. Once we began considering new names, it seemed like it took us forever to find one that captured the true essence of the school. We all contributed suggestions until we finally came up with American Institute of Alternative Medicine. With this new program we were able to offer more alternative healing therapies.

I was very excited about this recent accomplishment; what could be achieved next? I had always wanted to start a nursing program, based on a holistic foundation first of all, because nurses are so desperately needed and, secondly, very few of the programs are based on holistic sources of information. We kept putting it on the backburner for the same reason the acupuncture program had been on hold: we didn't know one iota of how to begin a nursing program.

Although it doesn't happen every day, the mother of one of our Asian graduates called me, wanting to sit down and talk. I agreed, and we met at a restaurant in Columbus. She confided that she was on the board of a school nursing program in another city, and they weren't doing well. It took me a while to realize she didn't want advice, which is why I thought we were meeting. Suddenly I had a flash of insight. "Can you excuse me for a minute?" I got up from the table and called Michelle. "Listen, I need you to get down here right now! I have so-and-so's mom here in front of me, and I think this is our way into a nursing program."

When Michelle arrived, all of us talked through everything. Michelle and I even went to visit the school and met the owner. As business owners, we recognized that he had mismanaged their funds, that the school was a sinking ship—and their whole faculty was screwed. And very soon, they would have no jobs. Michelle and I really felt bad for her, but we couldn't help. We were perfectly honest and suggested that she get legal advice and direction, to figure out how to get her investment back from the owner of that school. In the meantime, the opportunity to begin our nursing program was staring us in the face. We approached several staff members and asked if they were interested in coming aboard a new nursing school program with us. "Yeah, we'll come to Columbus!"

That was a godsend. In what could only be called perfect timing, we recruited some of their best people and still have a number of them today. One is our "Everything Dean" who is very with-it and navigates a sea of ever-changing regulations; she even came up with ways to get the nursing program underway. Since then, it's been a very successful program. Today, we have expanded into several nursing programs, and they are our most popular curriculum. I've sometimes wondered if our school would still be here today without them. But I have been shown repeatedly that the right people show up at the right time. And when I pay attention to what's happening around me, and listen to that little voice, it always steers me in the right direction.

Just when I thought things would settle down a little, more opportunities came knocking on my door.

My photo for the company I co-own,
American Institute of Alternative Medicine

Entrepreneur Leadership
Award (for AIAM) at the
2018 Ohio Asian Awards

*My art show
at Stonewall
Gallery*

*Having a blast playing bass with my band,
Wednesday Wine*

The fabulous cast from the play I wrote, A Bride for Kai

Always a wonderful time to be with friends from Ohio
Progressive Asian Women's Leadership Group (OPAWL)

Stepping off to lead one of the Columbus Gay Pride
Parades—always festive and energized

Cast from 110 in the Shade *with State of the Arts Productions founded by Quentin Edwards (this was the first time I got to have fun acting—I was hooked!)*

Chapter 20

Member of the Board

At the end of the National Women's Martial Arts Federation camp many years ago, I won a raffle. The prize was an all-expense paid package to go to the Pacific Association for Women's Martial Arts (PAWMA). A free trip to California? Yes! I thought it would be great to experience the martial arts conference and camps there.

My assigned roommate was on PAWMA's board. As we talked and got to know each other, she hinted at various details about the inner workings of their group, and her frustrations. What she shared sounded like simple business missteps, and I thought they could be remedied using business logic. As an entrepreneur, I see things in a different way. Things that seem obvious or like common sense to me are not apparent to everyone, and less so to non-business owners. I was surprised to learn that I carried a lot of experiences that others often find valuable. As I began asking questions, she felt we needed to continue our conversation and wanted to set up a meeting with the board. They were very concerned about heading toward being in the red. I agreed to talk to them.

The board consisted of a group of wonderful and passionate people. After introductions and light conversation, we began talking about some of their bigger concerns, mainly how to keep the group going while offering worthwhile conferences and camps in spite of rising costs and even higher expectations. I asked about their financial model and made some simple suggestions. They seemed impressed with my knowledge—the very things that I was doing with my business—and thought that I could be an asset to them. They offered me a position on their board, and I declined twice. Then, they all came to me on the last day of the camp and asked me again if I would serve on the board! I thought my living in Columbus, Ohio might be a conflict since they were on the West Coast, but they didn't see it as a problem. I finally agreed to be on the board under specific, limited terms. Later, I became the president in an advisory capacity.

There were nine board members in PAWMA. They are all martial artists. Because they were enthusiastic, they were all talking over each other. Changing this was the first order of business.

"Okay, excuse me! I can't hear anybody," I said in a loud voice. "I know you are all very passionate. Here's what we're going to do. We're going to use a method called 'divine governance.'" They were all curious about that. "Divine governance" is a term I learned in a non-violent communication workshop which they used to describe a scenario where everybody has a voice. "So," I continued, "we are going to go around the room and each of you will have an opportunity to speak what's on your mind. If you don't have anything to say, just say 'Pass' or 'Come back to me.'"

Because they could anticipate when they were getting their turn, that just calmed the energy right down. During that meeting, we had a wonderful brainstorming session and we achieved a lot more than any of us thought possible! What started out as a four-day board meeting was shortened to three days! I really learned a lot during my time with them. I enjoyed having the opportunity to co-create solutions and to contribute to the success of the martial arts camp.

After that experience with PAWMA, more opportunities began popping up. In 2018, the Asian American Commerce Group (AACG) called me. "We're calling to let you know that we have selected you to be the recipient of our AACG Business Entrepreneurship Award this year. We'd be honored to have you in attendance to receive your award." They mentioned it would be a formal event. Along with the mayor, there would be some other dignitaries and local celebrities attending, including the lovely Angela An of WBNS-10TV who would be the emcee. I knew all these names, and I'm like, "Whoa this is pretty big." So I said yes.

I didn't know anything about this association. I found out they're an economic group, with a lot of entrepreneurs from the Asian, Asian American, and Pacific Islander (AAPI) community. Well, it ended up being a very big deal. Nearly one thousand businesswomen and men were expected to attend. I was informed that all award nominees were to give a short speech. They sweetened the deal by encouraging us to invite ten people to the ceremony. I had no problem filling those seats, starting with my faithful business partner Michelle and her wife, my girlfriend at the time, and several dear friends.

The awards ceremony took place in a beautifully elegant ballroom. There were a dozen leadership award categories, such as Educational Leader, Healthcare Leader, Hospitality Leader, and even Lifetime Achievement and Philanthropy awards. Each nominee made a significant contribution to our community and city. I couldn't wait to hear from them. It was thrilling and encouraging to be around successful businesspeople from the vast Asian community in Ohio. I felt very much at home. It kicked off with a meet-and-greet cocktail hour which provided the opportunity to meet some of the other business owners. It was an incredible honor to be there. Many people introduced themselves to me. This added to a truly magical night and it made me feel like a rock star.

Each nominee gave their speech and accepted their award. As I was waiting to get up onto the stage, I stood next to a smiling, very unassuming gentleman who introduced himself as Dr. Arthur G.H. Bing. He was a nominee and a board member who had completed his residency at Riverside Methodist Hospital. He has been in the medical field for over fifty years. I had often seen the enormous, illuminated name on the front of the Ohio Health

Bing Cancer Center as I drove on the state route through the heart of Columbus.

"Dr. Bing, I actually think about you every time I'm on 315," I teased, "because I see your name on Riverside Hospital."

"Yes, and I'm so embarrassed about that!" he said, very humbly. Only later did I find out that his wife had been successfully treated for cancer there a number of decades previously. As a result, he became a major financial contributor to the hospital. In honor of his gift, Riverside Hospital named the wing after him. He's not the sort who draws attention to himself. He prefers to give quietly to foundations, organizations, and various causes near and dear to his heart. I befriended a lot of skilled and meritorious people through AACG, and he is one of them.

It was quite an honor to be recognized by such influential and prestigious peers; I was grateful to be counted among them. The focus was my culture and heritage! My speech touched on being in the presence of such successful Asian American business women and men. I thanked my grandfather who was for me the shining example of what a successful business owner looks like, because he started his business from scratch, just like I did. The impressive award was a gorgeous, sculpted flame of heavy, colored glass.

But there was one more surprise in store for me that night. After the ceremony, AACG asked me to join their board! That was a very unexpected honor and I was happy to accept. The Asian American Commerce Group is a collective of diverse supporters consisting of Chinese, Korean, Filipino, Indian, Indochinese, Pakistani, Hawaiian, Pacific Islander—you name it—who promote collaboration among the Asian American business community through education, networking, and inclusion. Everybody is extremely respectful. The connections run deep. AACG is always looking for ways to support Asian American businesses and businesspeople. During the first year of the pandemic, AACG helped business owners understand how to find PPP money and get business grants. AACG is also politically nonpartisan. During election cycles, panels are created which offer insight into each party's cause, their politician's passion, and who they are.

Being part of AACG has allowed me to make a significant difference in our community both locally and globally. At our Economic Summit, important dignitaries and ambassadors come from countries such as India, China, and Japan to discuss the economy, how it plays a role in their geographic locations, and how it affects us on a global scale. As a group, we are passionate and relentless in seeking ways to be bridge builders to better our community.

Around that same time, I was approached by several women from the Ohio Progressive Asian Women's Leadership (OPAWL). Another terrific group! I've been credited for being one of the founders, which surprises me because I honestly didn't know I was at the time. There was a conversation I heard about, after the fact, that went something like this:

One of them had mentioned my name. "Oh yeah, we need to get her on board because she's amazing!"

"Uh, yeah she is all that! But listen," said someone who knows me. "Let's not scare her off. Because we haven't even asked her if she wants to be a part of OPAWL!"

In the process of calling me to set up the meeting, I invited them to my school, AIAM. I told them I'd be happy to sit down and talk with them to hear what they had to say. On the day we met, they explained that OPAWL stands for connecting with the community of multi-ethnic and multigenerational women who are Asian, AAPI, and Native Hawaiian. Collectively we combine our resources to help support each other whether it is social injustice, discrimination due to sexual orientation, racial issues, or getting connected as a community. This vision resonated within me. I saw my role on the board as the manager or ambassador of fun! We collaborated with good food and entertainment, and actively sought Asian American Pacific Islander artists, speakers, book authors, or theater productions to support.

One offshoot was promoting the tradition of Chinese New Year, which is very popular among the local Chinese community. A lot of Chinese restaurants hired my Lion Dance team to perform the traditional New Year ceremony. I would dress up as the Buddha.

One can be really serious about social injustice and advocacy work, but it's really nice to have that balance with fun events.

I recall one event where a group of us went to listen to author Celeste Ng, who wrote *Everything I Never Told You*, a deeply thought provoking, page-turning tale about the cultural rifts in bi-ethnic families. She had a great stage presence and was very funny. I think we all got a copy of her book and had her sign it. We enjoyed talking with her; she was so sweet to us and was very supportive of our group.

Another time, we went to see Dr. Karen Korematsu, whose father, Fred Korematsu, ended up in the Japanese internment camp despite his creative attempts to evade the US Government. Fred Korematsu later became the iconic civil rights leader who was instrumental in winning reparations for Japanese camp survivors who lost their businesses, homes, and property during their WWII internment. Because the United States was at war with Japan, they wrongfully exercised extreme racial injustice and human rights abuses; over 100,000 Japanese were incarcerated, stripped of their freedom, family, finances, and livelihoods by the United States. A large group of OPAWL members went to the screening of the documentary *And Then They Came for Us* to support the writer Dr. Karen Korematsu. We got to hear the story of these events through her father's eye in the panel discussion that followed. It was an emotional night I will long remember.

After a season, I stepped down from an OPAWL leadership role to allow the younger women to take the reins. I was proud to have been part of the birthing of the group and happy to see that it continues to build under the new leadership. As organizations develop more racially diverse boards, I see more women, who are highly educated and experts in their field, add a tremendous amount of value. Even if I were the only woman on a board, I would feel the need to represent.

As a young child, I was representing Chinese Americans by being on teams, just with my presence. And as I became more confident, my voice followed my actions. I found people I could build relationships with and share a certain level of trust and respect. I think these bonds help add to not only a good life, but a life worth living to the fullest extent.

I also serve as a Community Relations Commissioner (CRC) for the city of Columbus. This commission consists of a diverse cross section of the people who inhabit Columbus: different ethnicities, gender orientations, races, religions, and cultures. I was granted the opportunity to be involved in discrimination complaints related to employment, housing, and public accommodation. Once a complaint is filed, a CRC Investigator will work with those people to gather facts, offer information, and guide them through a process. As commissioners, we listen to cases to determine whether there is just cause for us to take action. If there is enough evidence proving discrimination, the discriminating entity can be held accountable. The purpose is to reduce the occurrence of such incidents.

I was active with the CRC about one year before the Covid-19 pandemic hit. As the lockdowns were lifted, I learned that commissioners are expected to participate in most of the big important civic events like the Martin Luther King Day breakfast and other local events. It's important to be responsive and visible to the community by showing up. I enjoy participating in helping people who feel like they're being marginalized. I understand that feeling because I grew up experiencing racism and discrimination on several levels. I was on the committee which presented a "lunch and learn" series that would educate the public on different topics that were relevant to the larger community. For example, during the pandemic, we wanted to empower women dealing with domestic abuse. What we discovered was that there was more abuse but fewer reports, because the women had nowhere to get away from their abuser to make the call.

As part of that lunch and learn panel, which took place on a Zoom call, my segment was to offer self-defense suggestions that women could prepare for in advance. These suggestions were simple to implement if women found themselves in danger:

- Make sure to have a bag packed with the essential things you'll need to get out if you have to.

- Teach your kids to dial 911.
- Give kids some practical way to help you if you find yourself in severe danger.
- Make sure that all your important documents, and those of your kids, are hidden somewhere that will allow you to grab them quickly—along with some extra money and anything that helps you make an exit quickly.
- And if you do get into a physical confrontation, roll up into a ball so that you are protecting your internal organs. If at all possible, back into a corner which offers another level of protection.

I also taught a self-defense course to several hundred people. To gain such opportunities, I had to make myself available and visible. Networking with the other people of various organizations builds community. By knowing more people, I helped connect them in exponential ways.

Whether it's being on the executive board for AACG, being a commissioner, or VP for Stonewall, it's important to show the proper respect by attending and participating in the conversation and offering input. Otherwise, I'm cheating myself out of a rewarding experience—and cheating the board and society out of my perspective. I'm very proud of the opportunities to affect change in my community and in my board groups.

As the business grew, and my list of associations grew longer, I had more friends than I ever imagined I would. All of that made me happy and grateful. There were many beautiful experiences to reflect on. It's amazing to see how far I've come since that first job in Florida. I didn't miss being a graphic designer, but I enjoyed the creative process of painting. Were there other creative realms I should explore? Maybe those instruments of my grandfather's were tired of being idle, or maybe they were just a constant reminder that someone in our family once played music. What is a life without music? So many times, the unexpected things I had picked up and ran with had turned into far more than I ever could have imagined. What could happen if I picked up that guitar I had hung onto all these years and got serious about playing it?

Chapter 21

Wednesday Wine

As my community connections expanded, my interests evolved and changed. Community Festival, or ComFest as it is known to people in Columbus, Ohio, is the largest volunteer festival in the United States. It's exciting to see the performers, participate in workshops, enjoy food, and shop for crafts from street vendors. Some Columbus natives refer to Comfest as a "Party with a Purpose." Bands who perform at Comfest get "paid" with community festival coins to purchase food, beverages, or whatever treasures they find in the craft section. People volunteer to be part of this amazing event just for the bragging rights. It's an event that I look forward to every summer, not only because I get to work at the Gazebo stage, but because I get to talk to talented musicians from all over the Midwest region.

My love of music began when I was pretty young. It has been a comforting friend to me. When I wasn't participating in sports, I spent a lot of time in my room listening to albums by Carole King, Carly Simon, and classic rock songs. My older brothers listened to Motown, which really resonated with me as well. As a child, I didn't go around saying, "Yeah, when I get older, I'm gonna be in a band!" I didn't play an instrument. I would be with other children my age, and, on occasion, we'd pretend we were in a band. We'd sing into hairbrushes and play air guitars. That spark was always in my head, and it fit nicely with the fact that my grandfather was musically inclined. In my formative years, I was happy enough with the idea of listening to songs by other musicians.

The ability to play music was a slowly germinating seed that took decades to sprout. That seed sprouted and came alive in 2012 when a friend of mine asked me a simple question. "Hey, do you play a musical instrument?"

"I dabble with playing the guitar," I said. I had bought an acoustic six string from a pawn shop many years ago when I got my first job. I simply wanted to see if I could play it. I hadn't taken lessons, and I put it down a lot because pressing on the strings hurt my fingers. I kept it because I was determined to learn the basic chords and thought it would be cool to play some easy songs someday.

Soon after that conversation, my friend and I started having jam sessions which gave me a reason to learn how to play. A friend of hers was a singer. We invited her to join us. It wasn't overly serious; we were mostly having fun. Then, another friend of mine said something that inspired me. "We need a band to open for Bitch and Animal."

"Oh, we can open for them," I said confidently. And, just like that, we landed our first gig.

Bitch and Animal is a lesbian act, and they were extremely popular at the time. My friends and I put together a set list and began scouting for a drummer and bass player. I found a drummer easily. But we searched everywhere for a bass player. A week and a half before the gig, I couldn't find a bassist anywhere! It got me thinking, *Gosh, how hard can it be to play the bass? It's two fewer strings than a guitar!* So, I went to see a guy who taught bass. I explained that I didn't need to learn music theory or anything, I just needed to know how to play some simple songs and I needed to learn them fast!. That's what he taught me. I focused on learning the songs in the set of music we planned on playing as the opening act. We still didn't have a name for our band, however, we weren't concerned about that yet.

Some of my closest friends knew that Bitch and Animal were coming to town. The topic of conversation revolved around who was going to see the show. A group of my friends were hanging out with some people who were working on the show and the conversation took a surprising turn.

"Isn't it cool that your friend Helen is going to open for them?"

"What?" said my friend Lou. Then she texted me. "What's this I hear? You're opening for Bitch?"

"Yeah," I said. " It just came together really quickly..."

"I didn't even know you knew how to play an instrument!"

"Well, yeah . . . that came together pretty quickly too!"

This evolution happened at a surprising speed. Despite the fact that our playing wasn't the best, the show went great. Our group loved being a part of it. From that performance, we were asked to play for several different functions. So, we kept playing together. We named our band Wednesday Wine because we would practice on Wednesday nights and sometimes drink wine afterwards. We all loved classic rock music. Neil Young's "Ohio" and "Rockin' in the Free World" were favorites. When our lead guitarist moved away, we found another amazing lead guitarist named Karen. She's a talented "badass" who plays many instruments, including the violin (think "The Devil Went Down to Georgia").

After several years, I mentioned to the group how great it would be if we could get another bass player to fill in for me. I had an itch to do more traveling, and Wednesday Wine was regularly booked with engagements. That's when Karen found a bassist named Charity. She stepped in when I was away. Charity is actually a better bass player than I am, so it was a perfect solution to my desire to travel. It was great except that when I'd get home, I'd feel bad saying, "I'm back and you're out." Instead of going through all that, we increased the size of the band, and I switched to playing rhythm guitar. Rhythm guitar still allows me to sing background vocals to add harmony, which I love, without the pressure of having to concentrate too hard on playing.

My desire to try new experiences is a driving force, but, also, I visualize the best outcome. I visualize myself succeeding. I see events turning out well. I see the advantage of learning new things and often find many applications for those new skills personally and in business. And it's healthy for me to constantly challenge myself. I never really thought of myself as a risk taker. But after hearing people make comments like, "Why would you do that?" or "I can't believe you did that!" I came to realize that I am indeed a risk taker! What if I had said, "No, I don't play an instrument," or passed on the opportunity to open for Bitch and Animal? What if I had been too scared of messing up in front of a crowd of people to even try? Wednesday Wine would not have existed. Every performance was a risk, but also a chance to improve and share our playing with others. Part of it is being in the right place at the right time; the rest is recognizing the opportunities to grow as an individual.

My friend Suzie was one of the people who brought in entertainers and musical talent for the Columbus Pride Festival, Hot Time Festival, and other local events. She was also part of the entertainment crew at ComFest. I ended up helping Suzie, which eventually led to my assisting behind the stage: organizing performers coming into Columbus, arranging hotel accommodation, and getting them situated. And then I got to hang out with all these talented musicians. Wednesday Wine and I have been at ComFest almost every single year since the band started. All day we listen to great music and get to be a part of an amazing community event. The people who think volunteering and setting up is beneath them usually don't come back. But the dedicated ones come back year after year. So, at least four or five of our band members have volunteered every year. Eventually we were selected to play the main stage! This was great because of the visibility. Since that performance, we've been booked consistently in the city of Columbus. What fun!

It seems almost impossible to believe that Wednesday Wine has been together nearly ten years. Most of my bandmates make their living as musicians and have been in the music business a lot longer than I have. During the pandemic which began in March of 2020, while maintaining social-distancing protocols, Wednesday Wine worked most of the year to produce our first album of original music. Everyone in the band wrote and contributed songs for it.

I'm the least musical person in our band, and I even got to write the music and lyrics for one song! I'm very proud of this fact. I still enjoy playing music and being part of a band. Whether it was an unrecognized longing in my soul or a deeper desire to be more artistic, I appreciate the myriad forms of imaginative expression. Before too long, the creative muse paid me another visit.

Chapter 22

That was Quentin, Right?

Through AIAM I am put in touch with a wide range of people from all walks of life. Each student, client, and staff member has a myriad of projects they're juggling and networks they're part of. This is the fertile ground of opportunity. I never know when or where the next opportunity will pop up. Sometimes they occur where I least expected them.

One of the clients of our school suffered from juvenile arthritis. Her mother, Gwen, brought her in for massage therapy. As we were talking one day, Gwen shared that her son, Quentin, was living in New York and doing really well in theater. However, he wasn't doing well physically. He had a serious condition which necessitated his being on dialysis. As a result, he was moving back to Columbus. After he had returned and settled in, he told Gwen he was really frustrated with a lot of the local theater companies. He observed that they all performed the same old recycled plays and musicals, all with the same (largely white) people, and he desperately wanted more diversity.

"Well, why don't you start your own theater company then?" Gwen asked.

Quentin's response was, "I will." So, Quentin created State of the Arts Productions (SoArtsPro).

My friend and the school's director, Linda, mentioned that SoArts was looking for a bass player. I decided to meet with Quentin and audition for the job. At the tryouts, I realized they were looking for a classically trained bassist to perform with an orchestra. "Ohhh . . . I can't do that," I said. "I don't know how to read music."

When the music audition didn't work out, I offered the use of space at AIAM afterhours for rehearsal purposes. Quentin accepted, and I was thrilled.

"I kind of always wanted to be on a stage," I said.

"Why don't you audition?"

"Because I never went out for anything when I was in high school."

"Well, why don't you do it now?" he asked.

"Are you kidding?" I couldn't believe he was actually giving me—someone with no acting experience whatsoever—a chance to read for him!

"No. Give it a shot."

Quentin handed me an audition script. I was too excited to be nervous and read aloud from the page. He must have liked what I delivered because the next thing I knew, I was in a play called *110 in the Shade*. Talk about adverse! They allowed everyone to play different roles regardless of skin color or ethnic background. They refused to typecast. The cast was inclusive, and I was one of two Asian people playing unlikely parts—there aren't many Asian cowboys! I wore overalls and attempted to embody a deputy and midwife of the town, and the other Asian actor played the sheriff of an old southwestern town. It was a musical, too, which meant I got to sing on stage. What a blast! I met a lot of people related to the SoArts Theater. And, through the theater grapevine, SoArts quickly gained a reputation. People found Quentin's vision attractive and wanted to be part of it because we were so diverse.

Quentin and I became very close. He was like a brother to me. He often called me when he was on the dialysis machine. On those days we talked for a long time. During one of our conversations, I had an idea, and I ran it by him. "Quentin, I would like to get my reporter friend to do an article about you."

He was just thrilled when someone from a local magazine called to interview him while he went through dialysis. He really struggled health-wise, and, as much as it was possible, he never let that come between him and what he wanted to accomplish. SoArts was his focus. But he seemed very aware that his time was winding down. Before his interview was published, Quentin passed away. It was a huge loss to everyone who knew him. No one was more surprised than me when his mother, Gwen, called me.

"Quentin talked so much about you. He wanted you to be one of the people speaking at his funeral."

"Oh my gosh . . . I'd be honored." I had no idea he felt that way about me, or that I had touched him. That really meant a lot to me.

Not knowing Quentin for very long, I figured the funeral would be attended locally by a small group. Oh, was I wrong! Crowds of people stood outside the church. When I walked inside, I understood why. It was packed! Inside was standing room only. They had come from all over. At the front where the altar stood, a group performed dance routines. I should have guessed that where theater people gather, the funeral would be anything but typical. The pews were filled. Several people had been chosen to speak about Quentin and how he had impacted their lives. I talked about SoArts, Quentin's vision and what he'd created. It was obvious by the turnout that he was respected, loved, and very well-known in New York. Many of those with whom he had worked had come a great distance to pay their final respects.

Gwen, his mother, fought to produce the plays that Quentin had written on his list before he passed on. The vision for SoArts survived Quentin, and it became another organization near and dear to my heart because of Gwen and the people in it. She initially asked me to be on the board because of my connection with her son, but also because she felt that it was important that she and I stay connected. Gwen's a cool woman with a heart of gold. We go to lunch as often as we're able. We've continued to be friends, and I've grown to love her as a mother figure. I did everything I could to support her and Quentin's dream.

On the occasions that I worked with SoArts and acted in plays, I always felt like Quentin pulled us through some very difficult times. Some which defy explanation. Like the time we produced John Guare's *The House of Blue Leaves*. It's a popular play about a zookeeper from Queens, New York. It's set on the day the Pope comes to visit. I played the part of a nun. This play had a heavy emphasis on comedy. We were concerned about how well it would do in the box office because it was to be performed during the winter holidays. We didn't expect high ticket sales. That year the magazine *Playbill* phoned Gwen. They had been searching for a theater company doing *House of Blue Leaves* because the Pope was traveling to the United States. They checked every theater across the country and asked if we were performing the play and Gwen said the magic words: "Yes, we are." As a result, Playbill gave SoArts a whole bunch of free publicity! I think we were on our local station, WOSU, and *All Sides With Anne Fisher*! They talked about our theater company and how we happened to be performing this significant play about the Pope during the Pope's visit that same week. We had a surprising number of people attend our play, and it did better than we thought. It even got decent reviews.

Putting a play together isn't easy. There were times that we just didn't know how to line things up or how to make something work. We would be close to giving up. Just as we began thinking, *Now what are we going to do?* it would all miraculously smooth out and everything would be fine. And when these types of weird things happened, we would always say, "You know that was Quentin, right?"

"Oh, yeah. Oh, yeah."

It was a very cool experience. I never knew how one encounter would fold into the next, or what would come of being on stage playing a part.

Years later, I was in the audience at another event. A man I didn't know called out to me.

"Hey!"

Oooh, I'm in trouble! I thought.

"You were in *The House of Blue Leaves*," he said.

"Oh my gosh! Yes."

"I recognize you," he said. "You were hilarious as the nun."

"Thank you!" I said. Inside I was thinking, *Whaaat!?* Things like that made it even more fun to be a part of it all.

To be sure, there is a lot I don't know about the craft of acting. I wanted to explore that a little more and signed up for acting classes, and then a film-acting class. That led me to a small part in a short film where I played a juror. I also played a very small part as a nurse in a movie produced by filmmaker and director Stephanie West. This opened up opportunities to act in commercials for American Electric Power and Giant Eagle. I even acted in one with a speaking part. After that commercial began to air locally, I sometimes got text messages or calls from my friends. They would be brushing their teeth and, hearing my voice, they'd go look at their television screen and see me in the commercial. "Hey! I just saw you! You were in my living room!" So that was fun for nearly a year and a half. Once, I played a student intern for a Nationwide video tutorial for medical students. It was fun to challenge myself outside of my comfort zone.

Through a director search with SoArts, Gwen and I met the playwright Jack Petersen (a.k.a. Bob Weesner). That was the first time I met Jack and his wife, Julie. He'd been writing and directing plays for fifty years. I shared the story about the whole superstitious Ghost Wedding, and that, as a personal project, I was considering writing a short story, maybe even a play about it. Gwen had suggested making my story into a play. At the time I couldn't imagine how to accomplish such a task.

"I don't know . . . I don't know how to do that at all."

But Jack did know and said he was willing to help me. He had the credentials and had collaborated with many people to produce hundreds of plays. I ended up talking to him a lot. Finally I said, "Okay, let's go ahead and do it then."

It started out well. The play was titled *A Bride for Kai*. He recognized immediately the parts of the story that were funny and particularly the things my mom and I clashed on. "You can make it kinda funny in part," I said. "Because the story itself is funny."

But there were some things that Jack and I disagreed on. He wanted a whole lot more slapstick comedy. "Jack, I don't know . . . I don't like the slapstick stuff so much. It seems over the top." And I really resisted because it made me uncomfortable. To his credit, he eventually brought it down a bit. Even though I thought the wedding scene was way too slapsticky, I knew that he was a professional, that he'd been doing this a long time, and I decided to go with the flow. I felt like I might be overthinking it. But also, a part of it was that I felt protective of this story. Subconsciously, I didn't want the slapstick part to cross the line into making fun of me and my family, or mocking our culture. I didn't have any inkling that I was putting my whole life out there. And I wanted him to have the freedom to do the work, without hurting his feelings. But at certain points, I finally came out and said where I thought it was too much. Because it was a play, the story had to be filled in with dialog between the characters. So, even though the play was based on a true event, it wasn't word-for-word identical.

I learned a lot about what goes into the process of writing plays. Although we didn't always see eye to eye, I came to understand that plays take certain liberties. He had studied audience reactions for many years, and he was driven to make the play memorable. He did his best to make it marketable based on his decades of experience. Just like the time I spent with Quentin, that time spent creating a play with Jack was a gift. He mentioned several times how much he would love to produce and/or direct *A Bride for Kai*. Until a local theater could be found, he supported me in providing contest information locally and from around the country. One day I decided to put it out there. I submitted *A Bride for Kai* to every theater that seemed like a good fit just to see what would happen. Gwen and I arranged for a play reading. I even had auditions at my house in February. Even though all we did was read it on stage—it was the main stage! A bunch of people came to see it and we got great feedback. Then, right here in my own backyard, a theater festival contacted me about my submission. "Congratulations! We really like your play. We would like to have *A Bride for Kai* as part of the Columbus Black Theatre Festival." I won a contest!

The play was scheduled for its debut in June 2018 at Columbus Performing Arts Center (CPAC), where they have a couple of stages. We got a director who also played my girlfriend in the play. Because I was committed to teaching at a martial arts conference during that time, the director was really helpful in getting the people together. In an effort to present the story as authentically as possible, we tried to get Asian actors. Well, at that time in Columbus, that was a challenge. More than half the cast, including the fortune teller, the mom, and the actress that played me, had never acted before. I was just at a loss for making the cast completely Asian. So, we improvised. A white guy with an extensive acting career played the ghost character and did a fabulous job. Putting a play together is quite the process, but everything seemed to come together without a whole lot of effort.

In June, our play was performed as part of the Black Theatre Festival, along with several other plays. The day of the show was during my birthday week which made for a more festive celebration. The main stage at CPAC is big, with another stage across the hall. Productions occurred on both stages, and I was happy to see large crowds come out to see our play. They laughed in all the right places and seemed fascinated by the story. Despite our friendly disagreements, I was grateful to Jack for breathing life into a story from my past in a way that I could not have done without his help. And I'm forever grateful to Gwen who suggested it.

For a while, Jack and I discussed writing a trilogy based on additional stories from my life. The first story being A *Bride for Kai*, where a mother wanted to change the fate of her unlucky son by having a Ghost Wedding. The second tale was about a mother flying to Hong Kong and dying there after a fortune teller told me, "You're going to learn a lot about your ancestors." The third part was to be about some aspect of my present day life. Unfortunately, Jack passed away suddenly due to health complications.

To this day I'm glad that I had the opportunity to work with him when I did. I wouldn't have written the play by myself, but like so many other times, the right person showed up at the right time and opened that door. I just walked through it.

Chapter 23

Use Your Voice

On that dim spring night, after I abandoned my car and ran screaming across the street, the gunman had taken off on foot. I didn't know where he'd gone. But because the neighbor had not answered my knock at their door, I hid under the neighbor's car hoping the police would arrive soon.

Time seemed to standstill, but, finally, a police car arrived. Soon a helicopter circled overhead, casting a halogen spotlight beam into the yards of my neighbors. Search dogs paced back and forth, snuffling the ground trying to catch the scent of the man who had threatened me with a gun. I believed that this was the result of asking my business partner to call the police after I had called her to say I'd been held up at gunpoint. With the police now on the scene, I felt that it was finally safe enough to come out of hiding. As I tried standing on my feet, my rubbery legs began to buckle. *That's weird! What the hell's going on with my body?* Shock was setting in.

Police cars were parked on the street, their blue and red lights throwing light and shadows on house fronts. It was in that weird light that I recognized my neighbor Jim, a firefighter, from two doors down. I wobbled in his direction. Later, he'd tell me that he watched a guy park on the wrong side of the road, get out of his car, and pull his hoodie up. Jim was the hero who called the non-emergency police number. He didn't mind sharing the conversation they'd had.

"Hey, there's a suspicious guy in the neighborhood," he'd said. "So?"

But then he heard me scream. "Well, now I hear someone screaming."

"Oh! We'll dispatch a cruiser right away!"

When the gunman got out of my car and headed for his own vehicle, my neighbor hurried outside and picked up a piece of wood the size of a baseball bat from his yard to stop him. The gunman ran across the street and a few blocks down to High Street. Apparently, he was in good physical shape.

Meanwhile, my business partner told me later, she was across town thinking, *Oh my God!* and wondering where I was. At the office? At home? By the time she called police, they had more information.

"We've already got this and sent cruisers over there," they said.

It must have given her a little relief to know that the police were on it. Eventually, the bandit circled back around. Eyewitnesses said he jumped over a fence and nonchalantly attempted to gain access to his vehicle. It was surrounded by police.

"Hey, that's my car," he said.

When the police arrested him, they discovered he was wearing an ankle bracelet. He was already under house arrest! While the details were still fresh in my mind, the police asked me to identify him. I was still very shaken. The reality of being held at gunpoint was quickly sinking in.

"Listen," I said. "I don't want to be near him right now. I'm in shock."

All hope was not lost, however. The police had already found another witness. I believe she'd been held up and sexually assaulted earlier that same night! When they brought her over to look at him, she positively identified him.

"If he's got an ankle bracelet on, how come they weren't able to see that he had broken house arrest and where he was?" I asked the detective.

"Because he was only allowed to be home and go to work. The monitor only shows him going out of radar," he said. "The public doesn't know this, but if he goes out of radar (naturally assuming to work) he can come back into radar. They won't think anything of it."

"Wow," I said, surprised to learn they were not being monitored by GPS at that time. When do they think something of it?" Later it was revealed that he had held nineteen other women at gunpoint!

Karen, the neighbor who hadn't picked up my call, eventually looked out her window. Noticing all the commotion in the street, she came outside and then rushed over to me, with a horrified look on her face.

"Oh my God! What happened? I saw you called, but I said, 'I'll call her later.' I didn't think it was important!" (I've teased her about this ever since.)

By then I was shivering, and Karen invited me into her house. Pretty soon, the news reporters arrived. I didn't really want to talk to anyone because I was still kind of freaked out. While I was in Karen's house, all three local news stations posted people outside who were waiting to interview me. My first reaction was "I'm not going out there!" It had already been quite a night, and it was getting late. But then I started thinking about it. Another thing we teach in self-defense classes is to tell your story. Even though I really didn't want to, and I was very nervous and shaky, I felt a certain civic duty to share what I knew. By sharing my story, I could potentially help someone else, possibly even save their life. So I went out to talk with the reporters.

They asked their questions and requested that I re-enact the events, which I did. The next day, there were even more reporters from other stations. And then, I got a phone call.

"Hello, I'm Connie Shultz. I don't know if you know me, but I'm a Pulitzer Prize winning journalist . . . and I'm married to Senator Sherrod Brown . . . I don't know if that's good or bad."

"I know who Sherrod Brown is," I laughed. "And that's a good thing. I'm a Democrat."

Then she laughed.

"I'd like to do an exclusive interview and have the sole rights to your story."

"Well, the people from the news have already been here."

"Were they all local?

"Yeah."

"Well," she said. "I would like to have exclusive rights and do a nationally syndicated article about this because I know reading your story will help a lot of women."

National coverage meant it would be seen by many more people, and it would potentially make a difference in many lives. I may never know who, or ever hear the stories, but it made me feel good to know I was doing all I could to help prevent this from happening again. I quickly agreed.

We talked for about an hour on the phone, while she wrote down all the details. It wasn't easy retelling the events. It almost felt like this had happened to someone else. But because it was still very fresh, my heart hammered away in my chest. And in the back of my mind, I expected there to be repercussions from the bad guy. I pushed aside feelings of shame when I thought maybe others in the martial arts community would think I hadn't done all I could to protect myself. Or that they would have reacted better, more quickly, or had better ideas of what I should have done. But I reminded myself that what mattered most was that I was still here to tell my story and I had stood up to a bully with a gun. I believed that by telling it to a larger audience, that at least one other person—maybe many more—would be helped.

After the interview we continued our conversation:

"Helen, I'm impressed that you know the names of your neighbors, and you know their phone numbers, because that's non-existent now. Many people don't know their neighbors that well." Then she said something that really touched me. "I've also learned something very valuable from you."

"What's that?" I asked.

"To keep my cell phone on my body. Usually, I put it in my purse or handbag, or on my dashboard or whatever." So already, telling my experience had changed Connie's life.

After Connie published my story, comments from the public began pouring into her online site. There were responses from Japan, the Netherlands, Europe, Canada, and all over the United States. All the experts who had dedicated their lives to teaching self-defense and martial arts to women recognized that my whole experience, everything that I did, they were teaching in their classes. There were some remarks like, "Why didn't you call 911 instead of calling your neighbor/business partner?" and "Why did you use the name Darrin?" but Connie fielded those questions with responses along the lines of, "Let's not be critical of Helen. She survived. That's a successful outcome."

I would say 98% of the responses were "What an amazing story!" Some of the most respected and well-known names in the self-defense and martial arts community knew who I was. There were accolades from plenty of these experts from all over. And what did I gain from this experience? I had just received the highest honor. I was awarded my very life.

Months later, I attended a Thrive! business women's networking event, hosted by my friend, Mary B. One of their main speakers was Connie Schultz. Afterward in the Q&A, I raised my hand, curious if she remembered me. And I was chosen to ask a question.

"I don't know if you remember me," I said. "My name is Helen Yee."

"I know; I do remember you!" Then Connie told the whole audience the events of that night. "And now I keep my cell phone on me, ever since I heard your story."

It was so cool that she remembered me. I appreciated that she shared the critical detail about keeping your phone close. By sharing my story again, she had restated the warning to never go to a second location. I will likely never know how many lives were saved just by that message alone. It gave me a good feeling that the story went around the world and got a second play at the women's networking event.

I remember on the night I was running from the gunman how hard it was for me to find my voice. How many times had I shared that concept in our self-defense classes? "Use your voice!"

I even made a short video that I posted on YouTube sharing some ways that you can practice using your voice in case it ever becomes necessary—simply practice screaming in your car when you are alone. After the gunman incident, what I learned was that by screaming the police were sent! It was fortunate that my neighbor happened to be watching and on the phone. Reporting a suspicious man in the neighborhood did not motivate police. My running away from him didn't either. What got their attention and immediate action was sounding off in distress.

In a life and death situation, seconds count! We may think we know exactly what we would do if that situation happened to us. But until it occurs, you really don't know. If you freeze or panic, it could change everything. Being calm—fighting the butterflies—allows you to think clearly and quickly come to rational conclusions. In that instant, with a gun pointed at my head, it was not advantageous for me to attack him. What gave me the edge was being able to maintain a level of calm and focus to successfully escape. When I get out of my car at night, I'm more sensitive to my surroundings and any people who may be around me. In the end, it was of comfort and gratifying that my martial arts family said that I had acted in the best possible way. The words of Bruce Lee come back to me time and time again: "The best fight is no fight." This saved my life.

Chapter 24

The Spice of Life

"The better it gets . . . the better it gets."
~ Helen H. Yee

I said to my friend Robin, who was with me in Guatemala, "You know, I've always wanted to go hang gliding." We'd come across a group offering hang gliding flights. I could already imagine floating through the sky, with the sail rippling over me, the breeze in my face. I had flown plenty of times, but not like this.

"Have at it," she said. "I'll visit you in the hospital," she joked.

"Oh, stop saying that."

I was undeterred. Robin has always been a supportive comrade to many of my endeavors, but this time, she was okay letting me do this one on my own.

So, I went up a mountain with two Guatemalans who didn't speak much English. After he got me all strapped up in this tandem thing, he communicates to me that we are going to run off the cliff. "Just keep running, fast! Don't stop."

"Okay!" *Here I go.* I take off running with all this gear. It's light . . . but still . . . and he's right behind me. I'm running for all I'm worth, keeping my eye on the edge of the precipice which is coming up fast.

"STOP!" he yells.

What? Now? I'm on the edge of the cliff, looking down, but manage to keep from falling. I turn around and this guy and his buddy are fixing something on my strings which were attached to his shoe. Finally, he gives me a signal. "Okay! We're good."

The other guy waves me to come back to the starting point. "Do it again! Do it again!"

By this point, I was asking myself, *God, what the hell did I sign up for?* If this had happened to anyone else, I'm almost certain they would have called it off. I redirect my thoughts to the facts: *The problem is fixed. They caught it in time. Disaster averted. It's fine . . . . It'll be fine!* I am not easily rattled, and I didn't want wild speculations causing me to back out now. The sky was calling to me.

The second we get back in position, I run as fast as my legs will go to the edge of the cliff and leap into the air. The ground beneath my feet falls away and below me is a distant tropical landscape. I can see the tops of trees and birds hovering in the air. It is so peaceful and so quiet. The sandy beach looks like a white ribbon and beyond that, the wide open, sparkling blue sea. It's beautiful . . . stunning.

What made hang gliding thrilling was the most incredible sensation of flying like a bird. I sailed around up there for twenty minutes. It was even better than I imagined it could be. I glided near the cliffs, then out, and then my tandem flyer did some fun stuff. He spun us around and showed me a free fall; he really knew how to show a girl a great time! Some people say, "I would never go hang gliding!" They might even view such an adventure as reckless. But it isn't reckless when you have a copilot. It isn't reckless when someone does it for a living and offers you a chance to have a fun experience. The danger of falling off the cliff was kind of an afterthought. My focus wasn't on falling.

Then it was time to think about landing. They had driven Robin down to the edge of the water with her brother. I don't speak Spanish and my flight partner didn't speak much English, but he seemed to know enough to cover the basic concerns of his customers.

"How are we gonna land?" I said. "Hmmm? Land?"

"No worry! No worry," he said confidently. He directed our descent. When we came down, my feet literally just touched the beach. Fantastic flight and a perfect, soft landing. That's how experienced he was. Instead of dwelling on any negative outcomes, I focused on the fun. I focus on what it would be like if everything went right. And I expect it to go well.

I couldn't exactly say when I started thinking this way, but it likely stems from my childhood. Then, I was already the underdog; I had already been made fun of and been in a few fights just for being Chinese and looking different. Maybe I thought the worst had already happened. In any event, I reached the point where I didn't care. What anyone thought about me or what I did had lost its power over me. It was less about their approval and more about selecting the experiences that I wanted to have, trying new things, going in new directions, and challenging myself. I was like, "Hey, if I fall flat on my face, so what!? At least I gave it my best effort." Now, the only thing stopping me from doing what I want to do is just me.

One of the greatest lessons I learned from my dad was how to have fun in life. As a gambler, he understood that in the very nature of living you have to take a certain amount of risk. He wasn't afraid of risk and as I gained more experience, I saw the wisdom in that. In the larger picture, everything is a risk. Learning a new sport, driving a car, taking a class, beginning a relationship, or starting a new business. You always risk failing—but also succeeding. Without risking you will never know what you could have accomplished, how far you could have gone, or who you might have become. I threw caution to the wind a long time ago.

I'm always psyching myself up. I'm able to assess a situation rather quickly and weigh the risks versus the outcome. If that little voice isn't warning me off, then I just go all in, visualizing and expecting the best. Sometimes, there will be those things that we don't anticipate. You know, like in Greece. (Where, I remind you, if I had trusted my instincts and gotten my own bike, both my friend and I would have been fine.) While I admit to being largely fearless, I've finally learned to listen to and trust that inner voice.

When I was a regular jogger, I went for a jog on the Olentangy Trail near my home on a beautiful day. As I was about to go underneath the section near a bridge, I suddenly sensed trouble and heard something in my head saying, "Do not go any further." I turned right around and went back the way I came, which was so odd of me. To have continued on would have been reckless. Ignoring that warning voice would have been foolish.

Later that night, I heard on the news that a woman was sexually assaulted right there on the Olentangy Trail. That could have been me. Now, when I teach self-defense classes, especially for women, I explain the importance of giving ourselves permission to follow that intuition—"If your instincts tell you something's off, trust it." No matter how silly it may feel at the time, listening can literally save your life. It's remarkable how often that little voice is right.

As a younger person, I hadn't yet tuned in to that voice. Maybe because the parental voices were louder or more pressing. But even then, I listened to what my parents said and saw how it played out in my brothers' lives. It seemed to me that if they were giving good advice, then things should have been going much better for my brothers. Since the results didn't line up, my child's logic was to do the opposite of what my mother said regarding my culture. In hindsight, things did go slightly better for me than my brothers, but the way I went about it still cost me. Just going along with the crowd made me feel embarrassed and ashamed. I see now that trying to fit in didn't really serve me very well. The bullying I endured motivated me toward a positive result. That isn't true for everyone or every time. Bullying should never be tolerated. Those painful events made me want more, something better than what I had in that moment. It drove me to become empowered rather than be victimized. It doesn't have that effect on everyone. My brothers, and hundreds of thousands of other people, are proof of that.

It's funny, when I think back to the reasons for getting into martial arts, it was mainly to defend myself against those who were demeaning me. Despite the physical schoolyard fights with a few fellow students, I didn't really want to fight. What I really wanted was for the racism and bullying to end. I didn't want to attack them or retaliate. Even when racism was at its worst, I didn't instantly gravitate to fighting. Violence in and of itself rarely seemed to be the best solution. Martial arts training gave me more than just the skills to defend myself. I developed character, discipline, patience, respect, honor, virtue, and new patterns of thinking. Through martial arts, I was surrounded by people who held my culture in high esteem, which helped me see it in a new light. That helped immensely in removing the shame I had been carrying and helped restore me to my culture.

As I developed an appreciation for my personal originality and uniqueness, I began to love the fact that I was different. As I uncovered my individual preferences and my interests, I became comfortable with the real me. The particular combination of likes and dislikes, wants and needs, and talents, abilities, and insights make each of us who we are. None is better than the other. They're just different. Just as I am allowed to have my own voice, you are allowed to have your own voice too. We can have a difference of opinion. It's okay if we don't agree on everything—that's what makes us distinct from each other.

Difference is the spice of life. Differences are why we go to the movies, read books about other people's lives, and eat in different restaurants. The commonalities that unify us are that we want to be valued, we want to contribute and pursue happiness, and we want to be loved. Despite thinking in my younger years that I was an outsider in my own family, in the end, I can see how their contributions and influence played out in my life. My grandfather wanted me to do Tai Chi and Qigong with him. Now I'm in my sixties, and I've immersed myself in the passion of teaching those classes at workshops and conferences. On March 3, 2012, I earned an award from the Association of Women Martial Arts Instructors (AWMAI) for "30+ Years of Training and Dedication." Even though I did poo-poo a lot of my mom's pressure to embrace my Chinese heritage, she was right. I'm glad I've held on to as much as I did. Even though my mom and I watched Kung Fu movies for different reasons, it was because of Bruce Lee that I fell in love with martial arts. I'm grateful for his influence and all that he stood for at a critical point in my development.

In 2015, at the 40th annual Battle of Columbus/Martial Arts World Games, I was inducted into the Bruce Lee and Legends of Martial Arts Hall of Honor. People came from all over to attend the prestigious awards ceremony. Although my mother didn't think very highly of the little boy Bruce Lee, I think I could have finally convinced her to let it go that he threw *char siu bao* at her. If he hadn't made fighting moves look so cool, who knows where I would be today. She would probably shake her head at the irony.

In my family and original group of friends, I didn't have anyone pointing me to solutions for the bullying and racism that was going on. I did a lot of thinking and spent a lot of time alone. And though I would never wish it on anyone, adverse circumstances can strengthen us and help us clarify what's important. It can force us to consider alternatives, entertain solutions, and expand our thinking. In the moment, it doesn't feel like any of those things. As a source of real pain, we just want it to stop. But when facing ridicule and mockery head-on without allowing it to affect our decisions, we can become better, stronger, more resilient versions of ourselves. It is training for the future, helping to equip us for the many difficulties that lie ahead. It may well be the refining fire that solidifies our resolve "to show them." Think of all those wealthy computer "nerds."

While the bullying was hurtful at the time, it taught me a lot about people. There were those who turned the other way. But there were a select few who spoke up on my behalf. My classmate Lisa was one of them. She didn't even have to say very much. "You're being mean. Stop that right now." And it was over. The impact of her actions still reverberates to this day. Thank you, Lisa, for standing up for me. When she came to my rescue that day, it showed me that bullies are wrong. That even though they say things, often loudly, not everyone agrees with them. She made me feel like I was somebody worth defending. I had been "seen" by someone I admired, and her actions counted for a lot with me. I am still grateful. Once someone has done that for you, and you see how easy it is to circumvent a situation, you'll know what it means for someone else.

There was an event that occurred when I was in massage school. I had gone to the library to do research. In the back were these rowdy boys playing around and getting incrementally louder. I was able to ignore them until they finally became too loud for me to concentrate.

"Hey, knock it off down there. Be quiet."

They mocked me, and then one of them threw a book at me and hit my chair. That's it! I calmly closed my book, put it in my book bag, and purposely walked over to where they were standing together.

"Oh, here they come!" one said.

Now that I was closer, I saw that they were high school boys. Another stuck his foot out to trip me, but I reflexively dodged it. The well of confidence I had to draw from as a result of my martial arts training was a huge benefit that never failed me. Then I hit him so hard in the chest that he fell back against the books.

"Faggot!" he said and came at me. Then I saw that he was a head taller than me. I realized that he initially thought I was a gay guy.

"You want to take this outside?" I asked.

It was clear he didn't know what to do with me. I watched him exhibit a number of expressions, it was as though I could read every nuance that crossed his face. *Oops! I didn't know it was a female . . . and now she wants to take it outside!* I know what fear looks like, and he and his buddies had it written all over them. I walked straight past them and went to the librarian's desk.

"Hey, there's these guys in the back; you may want to check on them. They're making a lot of noise and trouble."

She cocked her elbows and put her hands on her hips. "Show me where they are."

I walked back there with her, and they saw me coming with the librarian. They quickly quieted and sat in their chairs pretending to be studying.

"These are the guys," I said. I stood behind the young man who tried to trip me and jabbed my finger hard into his shoulder with each word. "This one tried to trip me."

"I'll take care of this!" she said. I left knowing they weren't getting away with anything.

One day, I drove over to a bowling alley and went inside to pick up my niece and her friends. When I got there, I knew something was wrong. Instead of the usual silliness, laughing, and joking that such a group of girls engage in, they were very quiet.

"Shelly, what's going on?" I asked.

She shook her head and wouldn't look at me. And her friends were equally tight lipped. This really concerned me, and I wasn't going to let it go. I knew something had happened there, and I wasn't leaving until I knew what it was. As kindly and softly as I could, I repeated my request. "I want you to tell me what's going on."

Then she told me about some boys who had been making fun of them and pointed them out. All of those feelings from grade school came rushing back to me—about that boy who had picked on me relentlessly for no reason—until my big brother showed up in a car one day.

"Okay, thanks." I said. "I'll take care of it. You guys just stay here."

I walked over to the boys and basically said the same thing my brother said all those years ago. "Hey! So, you want to make fun of my niece over there? Why don't we take this outside, and we can settle this?"

Those boys couldn't even look at me, they were such cowards. Later I thought how amazing it was to have that full circle moment: my brother Tom had stood up to the bully for me, and then I stood up for his daughter against her bullies. Witnessing someone standing up for me showed me how easy it was to stand up for others. And though it has taken many forms, I've stood up to bullies all my life. Not only for myself, but especially for others. We can all stand up to racism in a variety of ways and be allies to those who are a minority, without having to do a throat punch or flying sidekick. We can stand in solidarity with our diverse brothers and sisters by speaking up, attending rallies, and even donating to organizations that promote ethnic communities and racial equality.

In this world that I live in, I continue to be grateful and optimistic because I have now connected to the strength and wisdom of my ancestors, which is deeply rooted in the essence of who I truly am. That spirit has inspired me to live the life I was born to live here in America. I am eternally grateful to them and to the many allies who foster racial equality. I will also be forever grateful to my martial arts family and Grand Master Joon Choi for the validation that was missing in my younger life. The philosophy, discipline, and physical and mental training from martial arts helped me navigate adulthood and brought me inner strength and awareness, peace, and a sense of who I am in the world, as well as many untold opportunities. Martial arts have been my saving grace, and in sharing my story, I hope it awakens countless possibilities for you to live your life to the fullest, with authenticity and without apology.

Author Bio

Born in Hong Kong and raised in Columbus, Ohio, Helen H. Yee co-founded the American Institute of Alternative Medicine (AIAM), where she is currently CFO, in 1990, after becoming a licensed massage therapist. As a graduate of Ohio Dominican University and a third-degree black belt in Taekwondo, Helen competed nationally  and internationally, is a two-time National gold medalist, and was selected as an alternate for the 1988 US Olympic Team. She competed on the US Taekwondo team in 1990, earning a silver medal in the first Women's World Cup Taekwondo in Madrid, Spain. In 2012, Helen earned an award from the Association of Women Martial Arts Instructors for "30+ Years of Training and Dedication" and was inducted into the Bruce Lee Martial Arts Legends Hall of Honor in 2015. She teaches Tai Chi and Qi Gong at martial arts camps, conferences, and seminars in the US and abroad. Energetic, friendly, and fun, Helen's goal is to support, inspire, and represent business women, lesbians, and Asians. With a strong background in business, Helen serves on the Accreditation Commission of Acupuncture and Oriental Medicine site visit team, for the evaluation of acupuncture and Oriental medicine schools across the country. She has participated as president for the Board for the Pacific Association of Women Martial Arts, executive board member for Asian American Commerce Group, vice president of the LGBTQ+ Stonewall Organization, original member of Ohio Progressive Asian Women's Leadership, and has served on numerous boards and committees. She has also been the recipient of the AACG Business Entrepreneurship Award.

Made in the USA
Columbia, SC
30 May 2022

61120368R00114